DOMINIQUAE BIERMAN

THE VOICE

OF

THESE
ASHES

RESTITUTION OR JUDGMENT

First Printing August 2023

Paperback ISBN: 978-1-953502-76-6
E-Book ISBN: 978-1-953502-77-3
Printed in the United States of America

Kad-Esh MAP Ministries
52 Tuscan Way, Ste 202-412, St Augustine, FL 32092, USA
www.Kad-Esh.org

Published by Zion's Gospel Press
shalom@zionsgospel.com
www.ZionsGospel.com

ZIONS GOSPEL
PRESS

Dedication

To my Jewish people, risen out of the ashes

I am the voice of the ashes of My people.

Then He said, "What have you done? The voice of your brother's blood is crying out to Me from the ground."

CONTENTS

Terminology

I WANT TO INTRODUCE A FEW IMPORTANT TERMS that I will use throughout the entire book:

YAHVEH

YHVH is the name of the LORD as revealed to Moses and used throughout the prophetic writings. It means "the I AM and the ever-present God." This name is often used in conjunction with the name ELOHIM, which is the name of the creator God.

ELOHIM

The name of the LORD when He is revealing Himself as the creator. Yahveh ELOHIM, "The I AM who is the creator."

In the beginning ELOHIM created the heavens and the earth. (Genesis 1:1)

Yah

Translated as God. Yah as in "HalleluYah." So, many times, I will use the word Yah instead of the word God.

Extol Him that rideth upon the heavens by His name Yah. (Psalm 68:4)

Yeshua

Yeshua is the original name of the Jewish Messiah, which the Father gave His Son through the angel Gabriel. Yeshua means "Yah is our salvation," implying salvation, deliverance, and redemption. You can read more about the importance of the original name of Yeshua in my book *Yeshua is the Name*.[1]

Torah

Torah is the Hebrew word for "instruction in righteousness," commonly called law. In this book, Torah only refers to the law of Yahveh in the five books of Moses and throughout the Bible.

Tallit

Tallit is a fringed garment worn as a prayer shawl by the Jews. The tallit has a special twine and knotted fringes known as tzitzit attached to its four corners. Tzitzit are to remind us of being obedient to God's Torah commandments and to be holy unto Him (Num. 15:38, Deut. 22:12).

---

[1]   Available at www.ZionsGospel.com

REPLACEMENT THEOLOGY

Replacement theology is a Christian doctrine that replaced the original Gospel that came out of Zion, Yeshua being a Jewish Messiah. In 325 AD, through the Council of Nicaea led by Eastern Roman Emperor Constantine, Christianity was established as the state religion of Byzantium, and it was based on replacement theology. This theology espoused that God is finished with Israel, and the Church replaces Israel and the Jewish People. The Christians inherit all the blessings given to Israel in the Hebrew Holy Scriptures, and the Jews inherit all the curses. The Jews are forever guilty of murdering Christ, although the Romans are actually the ones who executed Him.

The Hebrew Holy Scriptures (Tanakh) were renamed the Old Testament, and some of its contents were considered obsolete. Sunday replaced Shabbat as the holy day of rest, God's commandments were considered no longer relevant, biblical feasts were replaced by pagan feasts (e.g., Christmas replaced Sukkot), and the name of Yeshua the Messiah was changed to Jesus Christ. This led to a tragic separation from the Jews and everything Jewish and was a fertile ground for growing antisemitism in the church, leading all the way to the Nazi Shoah, and continuing until today.

SHOAH

Shoah is the correct Hebrew name for the Nazi Holocaust. Shoah means utter destruction, while Holocaust refers to a burnt sacrifice of pleasing aroma to YHVH, thus being an antisemitic name for the mass murder of the Jewish people.

3

ACT OF REPENTANCE

The context of this book pertains to private or public confessions and renouncing of sins on behalf of families, nations, churches, or governments, especially regarding specific issues like antisemitism, injustice, and crimes against the Jews. These can include mockery or anti-Israel and anti-Zionist feelings or politics. Acts of Restitution follow this.

Introduction

In Auschwitz, Treblinka, Sobibor, Majdanek, Babi Yar, Ukraine, and in many more locations, the blood of the Jewish people was either spilled or became ashes. This blood and these ashes went into the ground wherever they fell. But the soil never remains in one place; it migrates with the winds, rain, geological activity, and the passing of the years. These ashes, now mingled with the soil, have been scattered all over the world, bringing the essence of their poignant cry into your world, church, community, city, and nation.

About what did the blood of Abel cry out to the creator? About what are the blood and ashes of the Jews exterminated during the Shoah (Nazi Holocaust), Russian pogroms, the Spanish Inquisition, Christian crusades, Islamic terror, and much more crying to the God of the universe? And why should it matter to you, the reader? This is what you will find out in the pages of this book.

CHAPTER ONE

The Christian Connection

Since the year 2000, I have felt compelled to take as many people as possible with me to visit the death camps, especially Auschwitz. Having been an Israeli tour guide since 1983, I know how to organize and manage tour groups. By divine guidance, I found the right Polish tour operator who assisted me, and thus started my mission of bringing people to Auschwitz to have an encounter with the Nazi Shoah, the theologies and doctrines that prepared the way for Hitler, and the horrific fruit that followed.

Upon gazing at the mountain of hair, glasses, crutches, tallits, and children's and adult's shoes left behind by the victims, no manner of denial could remain. This horrific event really happened. The question is, why? How could this have happened in the modern twentieth century? Were we not an enlightened generation?

The words of one of the documentaries at Yad Vashem, the Shoah memorial in Jerusalem, brought even more questions:

Those who attacked their Jewish neighbors during this tragedy had been at the outset none other than good friends and Christian neighbors. Psychologists investigated this. How does a perfectly normal individual one day become a murderer and a monster a day later?

When I was visiting Sachsenhausen near Berlin, the concentration camp where all SS members were trained, a local guide said something shocking: these Nazi monsters who humiliated, tortured, and murdered Jewish babies, children, and adults during the day were also loving husbands and fathers after work hours. They made love to their wives, tucked their children into bed, and went to church on Sundays.

This puzzle does not get any easier to decipher unless one is willing to take the journey into the roots of many beliefs and theologies in Western Christianity. Unfortunately, thus far, not many have had the integrity and the willingness to take this journey to truth to expose and dismantle the monster that brought about the Shoah, the Christian pogroms in Russia (mainly during Easter and Christmas seasons), the Spanish/Mexican/Peruvian inquisitions and the Christian crusades to the Holy Land. Many interject that "this is a thing of the past" and has nothing to do with Christians today.

Except that the soil has migrated, and the cry of those Jewish ashes is now resounding to the Almighty from every nation represented by the United Nations and from every Christian pulpit and Islamic mosque that has neglected this important subject. The world is reeling and appears on the verge of the most devastating judgment humanity has ever experienced.

End Times believers call it the "Great Tribulation"; the Hebrew prophet Isaiah calls it "The day of vengeance for hostility against Zion."

> **Draw near, O nations, to hear, and listen, O peoples! Let the earth hear, and all it contains, the world, and all its offspring! For Adonai is enraged at all the nations, and furious at all their armies. He will utterly destroy them. He will give them over to slaughter. So their slain will be thrown out, and the stench of their corpses will rise, and the hills will be drenched with their blood. For Adonai has a day of vengeance, a year of recompense for the hostility against Zion.**
>
> Isaiah 34:1–3, 8

On one of my trips to Auschwitz, there was a very revealing photography exhibition. It had original pictures of Hitler's rise to power. Various images showed both Protestant ministers and Catholic priests extending their blessing and acceptance to the Fuhrer. The Christian leaders of Germany welcomed Hitler as a type of "savior" of his nation, one who could make Germany great and take her out of recession. By 1933, they all knew that Hitler hated the Jews and that his government meant hardship for them, but this did not deter the Christian leaders of the time.

Martin Luther, the greatest church reformer, had already prepared the way with his antisemitic writings and, after all, Germany was indeed the fatherland of all Protestants in the world. Hitler was inspired by Luther when he wrote about the Final Solution in his book *Mein Kampf*. Luther had already given his advice 400 years earlier.

Martin Luther wrote in his treatise *On the Jews and Their Lies* (1543):[2]

> What shall we Christians do with this rejected and condemned people, the Jews? Since they live among us, we dare not tolerate their conduct, now that we are aware of their lying and reviling and blaspheming. If we do, we become sharers in their lies, cursing and blasphemy. Thus we cannot extinguish the unquenchable fire of divine wrath, of which the prophets speak, nor can we convert the Jews. With prayer and the fear of God, we must practice a sharp mercy to see whether we might save at least a few from the glowing flames. We dare not avenge ourselves. Vengeance a thousand times worse than we could wish them already has them by the throat. I shall give you my sincere advice:
>
> First, to set fire to their synagogues or schools and to bury and cover with dirt whatever will not burn, so that no man will ever again see a stone or cinder of them. This is to be done in honor of our Lord and of Christendom, so that God might see that we are Christians.
>
> Second, I advise that their houses also be razed and destroyed, for they pursue in them the same aims as in their synagogues. Instead, they might be lodged under a roof or in a barn, like the gypsies. This will bring home

2   Martin Luther, Luther's Works: The Christian in Society IV, Vol. 47, translated by Martin H. Bertram (Philadelphia: Fortress Press, 1971), Parts 11

to them the fact that they are not masters in our country, as they boast, but that they are living in exile and in captivity, as they incessantly wail and lament about us before God.

Third, I advise that all their prayer books and Talmudic writings, in which such idolatry, lies, cursing, and blasphemy are taught, be taken from them.

Fourth, I advise that their rabbis be forbidden to teach henceforth on pain of loss of life and limb. For they have justly forfeited the right to such an office by holding the poor Jews captive with the saying of Moses (Deuteronomy 17:10) in which he commands them to obey their teachers on penalty of death, although Moses clearly adds: "what they teach you in accord with the law of the Lord." Those villains ignore that. They wantonly employ the poor people's obedience contrary to the law of the Lord and infuse them with this poison, cursing, and blasphemy. In the same way, the pope also held us captive with the declaration in Matthew 16:18, "You are Peter," etc., inducing us to believe all the lies and deceptions that issued from his devilish mind. He did not teach in accord with the word of God, and therefore he forfeited the right to teach.

Fifth, I advise that safe conduct on the highways be abolished completely for the Jews, for they have no business in the countryside since they are not lords, officials, tradesmen, or the like. Let them stay at home.

Moreover, since priesthood, worship, and government with which the greater part, indeed, almost all, of those laws of Moses deal, have been at an end for over fourteen hundred years already, it is certain that Moses' law also came to an end and lost its authority. Therefore the imperial laws must be applied to these imperial Jews. Their wish to be Mosaic Jews must not be indulged. In fact, no Jew has been that for over fourteen hundred years.

Sixth, I advise that usury be prohibited to them, and that all cash and treasure of silver and gold be taken from them and put aside for safekeeping.

Seventh, I recommend putting a flail, an ax, a hoe, a spade, a distaff, or a spindle into the hands of young, strong Jews and Jewesses and letting them earn their bread in the sweat of their brow, as was imposed on the children of Adam (Gen. 3:19). For it is not fitting that they should let us accursed Goyim toil in the sweat of our faces while they, the holy people, idle away their time behind the stove, feasting and farting, and on top of all, boasting blasphemously of their lordship over the Christians by means of our sweat. No, one should toss out these lazy rogues by the seat of their pants.

In brief, dear princes and lords, those of you who have Jews under your rule: if my counsel does not please you, find better advice, so that you and we all can be rid of the unbearable, devilish burden of the Jews.

Hitler followed Luther's advice and found a "better way" of getting rid of the Jews; he called it "The Final Solution."

CHAPTER TWO

An Altar of Ashes

*For I have eaten ashes like bread, and mixed my drink
with tears—"*

Psalms 102:10

On my tenth and last trip to Auschwitz in the
spring, I took only my team and no one else with me. We
went together to the field of ashes, where 1.5 million of my
people are buried. Besides the fact that there is a sign that says
"Ash Field," you would not know that this is the largest Jewish
burial site in the world! The Germans spilled the ashes from
the crematoriums into this field after gassing them to death
and then burning their bodies inside ovens. The field is covered
with soft grass in the spring, wildflowers growing here and
there, and one solitary tree in the midst of it.

I asked the members of my team to go and pray for one hour
around the field. Everyone was to find a private place, apart
from the others, to pray and ask Yah (God) to talk to us and

give us His heart and thoughts about this tragedy. As each person found their own corner of the field, I felt impressed to walk to the midst of it and to stand by the one solitary tree. As I reached my destination, gingerly stepping on the soft grass as if stepping over the corpses of my people, I heard the voice of my Abba, my Father in Heaven, the Spirit of Elohim whispering into my heart: "Lie here to rest on the Ash Field."

My instant reaction was one of resistance. I was horrified by this bizarre request from the God of Israel. "No, Lord, I cannot!" I cried back to Him. How can I lie down to rest on top of the ashes of my people? "You must," He retorted relentlessly. His voice was firm, and it commanded my obedience. Reluctantly, I took off my Latin American poncho, which represented my Sephardic Jewish ancestry, and laid it on the ground. I could not make myself lie on this ash field covered with soft grass and wildflowers without some protection between me and the ground. Then I proceeded to lie on this red poncho/wrap/blanket with tallit-like fringes all around. I lay there as quietly and "relaxed" as I could, obeying the voice of my God to the best of my ability. I was not prepared for what happened next.

In the stillness of the moment, I heard His voice resounding in my heart. His voice sounded like the heartbeat of Heaven. "This is your pulpit," He said. "From now on, you are preaching from here, from this ash field. You are the voice of these ashes."

CHAPTER THREE

Why Me?

For day and night Your hand was heavy upon me.
My strength was drained as in the droughts of summer. Selah.

PSALMS 32:4

I WAS SHAKEN TO THE CORE OF MY being. This is an awesome and terrible calling! How can I represent these ashes? How can I do them service? What does it mean for me to preach from here? Who would I preach to? What would I say? What am I supposed to do and accomplish? These and many more thoughts and poignant questions flooded my mind as the voice of my Father in Heaven, the God of Israel, echoed into every pore of my being. In answer, He gave this Scripture to me:

> Then Adonai said to Cain, "Where is Abel, your brother?" "I don't know," he said. "Am I my brother's keeper?" Then He said, "What have you done? The voice of your brother's blood is crying

out to Me from the ground. So now, cursed are you from the ground which opened its mouth to receive your brother's blood from your hand."

Genesis 4:9–11

I was lying on cursed ground! The blood of my Jewish people is crying to God from the ground of every nation where it has been spilled. The blood is crying out for judgment and vengeance to fall on those nations, peoples, and generations that gave their hand, instigated, or influenced the unjust murder of the Jewish people. It is crying for vengeance over those who did nothing to prevent this horrific genocide.

The blood is also crying against every nation represented in the Evian Conference of 1938, when no nation was willing to take in Jewish refugees and rescue them from the Nazis. Australia said it did not want to import a foreign immigration problem, the USA did not want to get involved, and the British had a restricted quota of those Jewish refugees allowed to enter the Land of Israel under the British Mandate (then called Palestine). It seemed to be that not one nation could escape the judgment of God for their hostility against Zion. The blood of His people is crying out from the ground, and I am assigned to be the voice of these ashes, the voice of their blood.

I remember how, on a previous trip to the death camps, I took people to Sobibor. Many people know of this hideous death camp from the movie "Escape from Sobibor." This place was a factory of death, but two Jews managed the impossible and escaped. To cover all evidence, the Germans dismantled the camp completely. However, the evidence of thousands of murders did not remain hidden for too long. As we were walking in the forest with our group, the trees looked very weird to me. They looked very thin and had an eerie red hue, as if they had drunk blood. Below most trees, I saw a strange white powder mingled with broken pieces of bone. This was everywhere! It was ghastly: human ashes mixed with bone fragments and so much of it! Then we arrived at a clearing full of uneven mounds; they were all unmarked graves, and they seemed endless. Suddenly, I heard dogs barking, babies crying, and women screaming blood-curdling screams. I looked around me, startled! Where was all this raucous sound coming from? We were totally alone in this place.

The terrifying noise continued. I called my husband and asked him: Do you hear anything? "Yes," he said. "I hear crazed dogs barking, babies screaming, people crying in terror, but there is no one here." I called on the others from our group who were further away and asked them: "Do you hear anything?" They said, "Yes!" We were totally puzzled, hearing these terrifying, heartbreaking cries coming from the ground all around us, but no one was there but us.

It was then that I realized that the blood of my people is indeed crying from the ground. Heartbreaking, terrifying, blood-curdling screams are calling to God from the ground for justice. This experience marked my life and the lives of all those who heard it with me. The cry of the blood cannot and will not be ignored any longer!

I was still lying on the Ash Field when I remembered this event in Sobibor. Realizing that I am to be the voice of this crying blood, the voice of these ashes, I asked silently:

"Why me, Abba?" Then His shalom came over me, and I prayed:

The blood of my Jewish family is crying for revenge, and I cry for holy revenge, so that what the devil meant for evil will be turned for good. I ask that every drop of Jewish blood, every one of those ashes that are crying out, will become a soul for Your kingdom.

I did not know how this would happen, though I knew that this would not be any kind of cheap grace poured out on the hostile nations, mostly Christian nations, worldwide. This would be a very costly grace that would demand:

Restitution

I also realized that if restitution would not be granted the only thing for most Christian or formerly Christian nations to expect is:

Judgment

> **For Adonai has a day of vengeance, a year of recompense for the hostility against Zion.**
>
> **Isaiah 34:8**

CHAPTER FOUR

Restitution or Judgment:
That is the Question

Now there was a famine in the days of David for three years, year after year, so David sought the face of Adonai. Adonai replied, "It is because of Saul and his bloody house, for he put the Gibeonites to death."

2 SAMUEL 21:1

THIS CHAPTER OF THE REIGN OF DAVID CONTAINS a perfect example of the need for restitution. First, we must understand that judgment for innocent bloodshed may take place long after the event and affect later generations and governments. David was not to blame for breaking the covenant with the Gibeonites by murdering them; King Saul, David's predecessor, was the guilty party. Yet David was suffering for the sins he inherited. Sins and curses because of past wrongs can be visited up to ten generations later.

The Ammonites and Moabites that refused to help Israel in the desert were punished for ten consecutive generations!

> "No Ammonite or Moabite is to enter the community of Adonai—even to the tenth generation none belonging to them is to enter the community of Adonai forever— because they did not meet you with bread and water on the way when you came out from Egypt, and because they hired against you Balaam son of Beor from Petor of Aram-naharaim to curse you."
>
> Deuteronomy 23:4-5

King David understood that the only way out of the curse his predecessor left him was through an Act of Restitution. The famine would never break, and all of Israel could die unless the curse for the murder of the Gibeonites was broken. He turned to them to seek to appease them.

> So the king summoned the Gibeonites and spoke to them. (Now the Gibeonites were not of Bnei-Yisrael but a remnant of the Amorites; however, Bnei-Yisrael had sworn a covenant with them. Yet Saul had tried to eradicate them in his zeal for Bnei-Yisrael and Judah.) David asked the Gibeonites, "What should I do for you? How may I make atonement so that you would bless the inheritance of Adonai?"
>
> 2 Samuel 21:2-3

In this case, the Gibeonites demanded blood for blood.

> The Gibeonites said to him, "It is not a matter of silver or gold between us and Saul or his house; nor is it our right to put any man to death in Israel." "Whatever you say, I will do for you," he said. Then they said to the king, "The man who consumed us and plotted against us to annihilate us from remaining in any of Israel's territory, let seven men of his sons be given over to us and we will hang them up before Adonai at Gibeah of Saul, Adonai's chosen." "I will give them over," the king said.
>
> 2 Samuel 21:4-6

Besides Mephiboshet, the disabled son of Jonathan, David complied, and he handed these seven men from the house of Saul to satisfy the Gibeonites.

> and he gave them into the hands of the Gibeonites. So they hanged them on the hill before Adonai, so that all seven fell together. They were put to death during the days of harvest, at the beginning of barley harvest.
>
> 2 Samuel 21:9

What is most revealing is the response of Heaven to this difficult act of righteous restitution. The curse broke, and YHVH's hand was moved to answer prayer on behalf of the land!

> So they buried the bones of Saul and his son
> Jonathan in the country of Benjamin in Zela, in the
> tomb of his father Kish. They did all of what the
> king commanded. Afterward, God was moved by
> prayer for the land.

> 2 Samuel 21:14

When righteous acts of restitution take place, curses break, and prayers are answered. In a later chapter, I will explain why acts of restitution are mandatory concerning the Jewish People and why this needs to be done by the Christians and nations of our generation even if you have received forgiveness due to Yeshua's sacrifice for your sins or if you personally are not to blame for any Antisemitism. King David was not to blame for the sin committed against the Gibeonites, but he needed to act to overturn the curse that he had inherited.

In the last chapters of this book, you will see what acts of restitution can be done by believers in Messiah.

Restitution means to make reparations, to repay what was stolen or damaged plus interest; to do good where an individual or their ancestors did evil to someone. When that someone is a Jew, it is even more serious, as only the natural descendants of Abraham, Isaac, and Jacob are promised the following:

> "I will bless those who bless you, and him who
> dishonors you I will curse, and in you all the families
> of the earth shall be blessed."

> Genesis 12:3 ESV

I call this the *Key of Abraham* that opens or closes the blessing for individuals, families, communities, churches, cities, and nations. This ancient key never fails to open or close doors for blessing or curse. The blood of the Jewish people crying out from the ground is a disaster waiting to happen anywhere in the world where antisemitism exists, including the hatred against the Jews or the present-day State of Israel.

This includes all the nations represented by the United Nations that have constantly bashed Israel unjustly. It includes every church that espouses replacement theology, pride, or a condescending attitude against the Jews or the State of Israel. It includes every government that opposes the restoration of the Jewish people back to every part of their covenant land, every mosque that spews venom and hatred against the Jews, and every family where Jews are made light of or mocked.

The wrath of Yah (God) will be poured out everywhere unless there is heartfelt repentance followed by restitution. Though the blood of Messiah atones for all sins when there is true repentance, doing good where evil was done is mandatory. Restitution is the fruit of true repentance. Nothing else will do!

The end-time revival and harvest of souls will be very, very costly due to the terrible hatred of Jews throughout the ages, mainly by Christians and now Muslims. It will be so costly that the most venerated Christian theologies will be dismantled until Christianity, as created by Roman Emperor Constantine, is no more and every child of God returns to the Jewish Messiah and to the gospel made in Zion as preached by the Jewish apostles of the first century.

Repent, therefore, and return—so your sins might be blotted out, so times of relief might come from the presence of Adonai, and He might send Yeshua, the Messiah appointed for you. Heaven must receive Him, until the time of the restoration of all the things that God spoke about long ago through the mouth of His holy prophets.

Acts 3:19–21

CHAPTER FIVE

From the Ash Field to the Mine Field

Save me from the lion's mouth.
From the horns of the wild oxen rescue me.

PSALMS 22:22

MY HUSBAND AND I WERE INVITED TO A special meeting on the Mount of Olives between Israeli and Polish pastors. We were part of the Israeli pastors' delegation. After a time of sweet and neutral joint worship, the leaders of the meeting suggested we take communion to show our unity with the Polish pastors. During the meeting, no issues were addressed, no discussion about the role Christians in Poland played during the Nazi Shoah, no sensitive issues were dealt with, no repentance, no restitution, no forgiveness, and nothing "controversial" was mentioned. The fact that most of the six million Jews were exterminated in death camps all over Poland was not even mentioned, let alone the blood guilt. This was only a "nice" Christian meeting.

The elements of communion were passed around. As I held them in my hands, the Spirit of God asked me a startling question: "Dominiquae, what are you doing?" "I am taking communion with my brethren, Lord," I answered in surprise. "Communion is a covenant meal," He said firmly. Then I understood why He stopped me. I rose to my feet and said to all, "Communion is a covenant meal. If so," I said, turning to my Polish brethren, "my pulpit is open to you. Will your pulpit be open to me (as a Jewish prophet) as well?" They were taken aback. Then they answered truthfully: "We are not ready for this yet." Then I said, "Then I am not ready to take communion with you."

My Israeli brethren sneered at me and began to put me down for seemingly offending our Polish guests this way. Who did I think I was, as a woman, to do something so "out of order"? But I knew that I was standing as the voice of the ashes of my people, doing the will of Yah. One of the Israeli pastors from the city of Beersheva confronted me accusingly, saying, "Woman! Submit to your husband!" My husband, Rabbi Baruch, was standing by my side, and he replied: "She is submitted; now, what is your problem?"

I caused a serious stir that day. The Israelis were uncomfortable; they did not want to deal with the crux of the matter. To this day, most Messianic ministers avoid confronting Christians or Christianity with replacement theology or antisemitism. They prefer acceptance and popularity, but I cannot afford it. I am the voice of these ashes, and I will give an account to them and the only Judge of all flesh. What matters is that I am popular with Him.

The Polish pastors were embarrassed, but it made them think. Some came to thank me later.

On the way back home, satan began to plague me with remorse. Maybe I should have been more diplomatic, more careful, and less offensive. We were inside our van, driving back home from Jerusalem, when I was having second thoughts. All of a sudden, Ruach Elohim fell upon me, and His voice told me something I will never forget:

"Even if you offended them, it is not comparable to six million Jews exterminated!"

I began to scream and weep uncontrollably. My husband had to pull the van to the side of the road as everything was shaking.

Then I saw *Yeshua*! He was dressed in His tallit, and He knelt down to kiss my feet, saying, "Forgive My people; they should be kissing your feet." I was shocked and embarrassed to see Yeshua kneeling down, and I tried to stop Him. He rose up to His feet and commanded me to look ahead of me. I was standing in front of a large black minefield. He said: "This is the minefield of Christianity. It is blackened by the quantity of mines in it. I want you to walk across the field. Many have tried before you, but they have either died, been wounded, or pulled back. But I want you to cross it. Do not skirt around the mines. There are too many, and you cannot avoid them exploding. But when they explode, I will heal you *every time!*"

CHAPTER SIX

The Dividing of the Mine Field

And He will put the sheep on His right,
but the goats on His left.

MATTHEW 25:33

I REALIZE THAT SOME OF YOU MAY FEEL offended by my message here. I understand that people are "touchy" about what they consider "sacred." There are "sacred cows" in every religious system that no one would dare touch, and Christianity is no different. I hope you will look past all your trigger points and into the Holy One of Israel and the Spirit of Truth. Most people are afraid of the truth because they say "the truth hurts." But I see truth as medical alcohol or peroxide. These are both agents of healing like truth is. if you have a wound or an infection, putting in some medical alcohol may sting terribly, not because of the alcohol itself, but because the infection hurts. Some infections, if untreated, may cause gangrene, rot, and ultimate death. Antisemitism stemming from the deathly doctrines of Replacement Theology Christianity is a dangerous spiritual infection. It is so intertwined with the entire religious system of Christianity because it is the foundation of it. Please keep in mind that Yeshua, the Messiah and Savior was not a Christian; He is a Jew. And He did not bring Christianity to the world; Emperor Constantine did. Yeshua said:

> **I am the way, the truth and the life. No one comes to the Father but through Me.**
>
> **John 14:6**

Notice that He did not say: No one comes to the Father but through Christianity or belief in the doctrines and tenets of Christianity or any other religious system, but only "through Me." He is a Jewish Messiah, and all the doctrines of Faith in Messiah should be "Kingdom doctrines" based on the Hebrew Holy Scriptures interpreted by the Holy Spirit. This is why Yeshua constantly quoted from the original Hebrew Bible, as did Paul and everyone else. Once the Holy Spirit comes inside us, he helps us interpret the Word of God. And I assure you that the Holy Spirit would never contradict the Word of YHVH. However, many Christian doctrines do so and favor the traditions of fallen angels and men to Biblical traditions. What is called Antisemitism today was not born in a vacuum but in the fertile soil of Christianity, established as the religion of the Roman Empire from the 4th century and on. If you love religion more than truth, this book is not for you. If you prefer tradition to obedience to God and His Word, then you will get offended. I hope you will keep on reading and love truth more than lies. For one lie caused the Fall of Man, and satan is the father of all lies; and Yeshua, the Jewish Messiah who is not a Christian, is the Truth. I hope you choose Him above religion.

You shall know the truth and the truth will make you free.

John 8:32

To help you with any questions this chapter or this book may raise, I wrote a comprehensive book called *The Identity Theft*[3] about religious antisemitism; please read that book as the truth in it will set you free, and get you acquainted with Yeshua the King of the Jews in the fullness of His identity. Once His identity is restored, yours will be restored as well. Religion comes from the forbidden tree of knowledge of good and evil, but true faith in Messiah comes from the Tree of Life. If Christianity had been from the Tree of Life, it would not have been the poisoned soil of most antisemitic acts and Jewish hatred since the 4th century and on.

A good tree cannot produce bad fruit, nor can a rotten tree produce good fruit. Every tree that does not produce good fruit is chopped down and thrown into the fire. So then, you will recognize them by their fruit.

Matthew 7:18–20

---

[3]   Available at www.AgainstAntisemitism.com

Historical and modern-day antisemitism, including the Crusades, Spanish Inquisition, pogroms, expulsions of Jews from all over Europe, and even the Nazi Shoah itself, have been in the name of Christ, and it is the fruit of Christianity. Therefore, Christianity is not Yeshua; it is not the Gospel that came from Zion. It is not the Tree of Life. It is a mixed tree or system; thus, it is the poison tree of knowledge of good and evil. It does not only kill Jews, but it kills you as well. Whatever is of value in your faith is not Christianity; it is His Word, the truth, the Gospel, etc. But Christianity is mixed with many other things, mainly pagan and Roman, and certainly anti-Biblical and ungodly things.

Christian doctrines full of replacement theology, pagan traditions, and antisemitism are likened unto deathly and dangerous mines. I call this the five-headed monster or the Anti-MESITOJUZ principality.[4]

Yeshua told me that I was to "cross the minefield of Christianity." In Hebrew, the word for "to cross" means to divide. As the voice of the ashes—by my preaching, singing, writing, and ministering—I am to bring a distinct line of division between Christians who will repent from replacement theology, the pagan feasts, and roots of Christianity that lead to antisemitism and those who will reject this prophetic end-time message.

I was to present this message before all Christians, as written in many of my books, such as *The Healing Power of the Roots,*

---

[4]   Anti-Messiah, Anti-Israel, Anti-Torah, Anti-Jewish, Anti-Zionism. For more information about the subject, order *The Identity Theft* at www.Against-Antisemitism.com

The MAP Revolution, The Identity Theft, and more. Those who would repent and make restitution to Israel and the Jewish people through their prayers, giving, and actions would obtain great grace and mercy. They will be vessels of fire for the third-day revival (third millennium) and harvest. Those who would reject this end-time prophetic message would be judged together with the rest of the unrepentant world for their arrogant and hard hearts.

> **True enough. They were broken off because of unbelief, and you stand by faith. Do not be arrogant, but fear— for if God did not spare the natural branches, neither will He spare you.**
>
> Romans 11:20–21

In another passage of scripture, Yeshua tells us that He will separate entire nations one from the other; the sheep nations He will put on his right and the goat nations on his left. The sheep nations will inherit the Kingdom of God and eternal life; the goat nations will go to eternal destruction. The determining factor is how the nations treated "the least of His brethren." Since Yeshua is a Jew and He was speaking this parable about the nations to His Jewish disciples in His Land, Israel, it makes sense that "the least of His brethren" are the Jewish People. The way the nations have treated the Jews will determine their eternal destiny. Most Antisemitic acts, murders, humiliations, and expulsions have happened in Christian nations.

And answering, the King will say to them, 'Amen, I tell you, whatever you did to one of the least of these My brethren, you did it to Me.'

Matthew 25:40

CHAPTER SEVEN

A Family Treasure

ON ONE OF OUR FIRST TRIPS TO AUSCHWITZ, I took a group of Swiss Germans and Americans with me. First, we went to an area called Auschwitz 1, which used to be a concentration camp and a prison. Later in the day, I took them to Auschwitz 2 (also called Birkenau), which was solely a death camp, a factory of death.

All the exhibits are in Auschwitz 1, and among them are the crematorium ovens. As we approached the ovens, I stood next to one of them, facing the group. This was a very solemn moment for all of us. Then I began to speak: "Had I been alive at the time of the Nazi Shoah, I would have been among these ashes inside this oven. I do not know why God chose that I would be born later. So then, I have a job to do in my generation: to prevent it from happening again. This is why I brought you here."

There was a holy hush; here and there, you could hear a muffled sniffle. Then a tall Swiss German lady came forward and approached me; she was carrying a bulky package in her arms. "Is this a very holy place for you?" she asked. "Extremely," I said. "This is the largest Jewish cemetery in the world. One and a half million of my people were burnt to ashes here."

Everyone was very quiet as she proceeded to hand me her bulky package. "This is all my family jewelry, inherited from my German family for many generations. God told me to bring it to you and hand it to you here. This is my family's restitution for what we Germans did to your people. I ask you to forgive us in the name of your Jewish people."

I was stunned and even shocked by this unexpected turn of events. My hands clutched this heavy family treasure reluctantly. I had no other choice but to humble myself and receive the package. I was too numb to feel anything, though; in my mind, I was not sure if I even had the right to receive this restitution treasure. Furthermore, could I release forgiveness on behalf of the ashes of my people? I found myself saying, "I forgive you and your family," as I heard the sobs of many others in the group.

Later, I would take this family treasure and distribute it to other Jews as the Spirit of Adonai would show me. I could not keep all this for myself. One of the recipients was my father-in-law. He had lost his leg as a Jewish fighter with the British against the Nazi German army. He was advanced in years and was sitting in a wheelchair when I showed him the collection of rings that were part of the package. I told him the story and then asked him to choose one ring. He broke into tears as he put the chosen ring on his pinky finger. That day, his heart softened toward the Christians, and he eventually opened up to receive the Jewish Messiah.

CHAPTER EIGHT

The Cry of the Blood

WHAT IS THE BLOOD CRYING? WHAT IS IT saying? What is it calling? And must these cries be satisfied? Does the Bible have an answer, even a very clear answer?

> ... eye for an eye, tooth for a tooth, hand for hand, foot for foot, burn for burn, wound for wound, blow for blow.
>
> Exodus 21:24–25

Yes, the blood of my Jewish people is crying for justice, and biblical justice is not a Christian thing; it is a legal right, and it must be satisfied exactly as written above. Do you know how many eyes of my people have been gouged, how many teeth were extracted to remove the gold from the fillings after the people were murdered in the gas chambers? Imagine that much of this gold extracted from the teeth of the dead is still lying inside safes in Swiss banks. That gold is also required; the teeth are required.

Do you know how many Jews were widowed and orphaned throughout history, and all in the name of Christ, during the Christian crusades, the Spanish Inquisition, the Mexican, Peruvian, and other Latin American inquisitions, Russian and Ukrainian pogroms, especially during the Christmas and Easter seasons, during ruthless expulsions and uprooting of Jewish villages all over Europe, including England, France, and during the Nazi Shoah? The blood is crying out about that too.

> **You must not mistreat any widow or orphan. If you mistreat them in any way, and they cry out to Me, I will surely hear their cry. My wrath will burn hot, and I will kill you with the sword. So, your wives will become widows and your children will become orphans.**
>
> **Exodus 22:21–23**

But not only does the blood cry about the loss of life, but even the properties and possessions that were plundered. Every time Jews were plundered, their possessions confiscated, and their livelihood destroyed, their lives were ruined and made into a misery of poverty. The blood is calling from the ground for justice and restitution.

> **For thus says Adonai-Tzva'ot, He has sent me after glory to the nations that plundered you—because whoever touches you touches the apple of His eye— 'For behold, I will shake My hand against them, and they will be plunder to their servants.' Then you will**

know that Adonai-Tzva'ot has sent me.

Zechariah 2:12–13

When I visited Bitola, known during the Ottoman Empire as Monastir, in North Macedonia in 2018, I was amazed to find the beautiful house my family owned before the Second World War. It was a palatial mansion standing in the middle of the main city square, and it is still called the Albala House, Albala being my maiden name from my father's side. Albeit the last Albala in the city had been taken to the death camp of Treblinka, where he became ashes, like all those living in Monastir during the war.

When I looked at the freshly painted, historical mansion being turned into a hotel, I asked to visit it and talk with the new owner. He is a lawyer and was kind enough to meet me and let me visit it. I felt deep emotion as I recognized the Jewish motifs on the exterior walls. They were restored by law to look exactly the same as they had looked in 1942. This house belonged to a part of my family, yet no one paid my relatives for that palace. The family, like all other Jews, were plundered, and my last living relatives in that city were sent to their death by the Nazis. Their blood is also crying "Justice!" from the ground.

But could this still affect the nations now, even after the Messiah has come? Isn't His blood sufficient to satisfy all justice? The blood of Yeshua only satisfies the offenses against the God who created us. He forgives those who repent of their crimes and put their trust in Him, but forgiveness by humans is another matter; this takes another course, the course of restitution, and often a punishment for offenses. Let me explain:

A rapist may repent of his sins and receive forgiveness from the creator because of the blood sacrifice of His Son, the Jewish Messiah. However, this would not absolve him from going to prison and doing a considerable amount of time for his crime. The wronged woman who was abused deserves justice, and even if she forgives him, the law might not.

All the way until the end of the Holy Scriptures in the book of Revelation, the slain are crying out for justice, and the slain will not be denied. Their blood is crying from the ground. We could say these are martyrs of Yeshua, but the Scriptures only mention that they were killed because of the word of God. Many Jews have been murdered and their synagogues burned for believing the Torah: The Torah is the first five books of the Bible, and they are the word of God. In fact, the Nazi Shoah started by burning synagogues and Torah scrolls containing Yah's commandments and, among them, "You shall not murder."

> When the Lamb opened the fifth seal, I saw under the altar the souls of those slaughtered for the sake of the Word of God and for the witness they had. And they cried out with a loud voice, saying, "O Sovereign Master, holy and true, how long before You judge those who dwell on the earth and avenge our blood?"
>
> Revelation 6:9–10

Dealing with blood guilt takes us through acts of repentance toward God and restitution toward men. Only these actions can comfort the blood of the innocent who were slain. That is why acts of restitution are so important; they can release bondages and break through personal, family, and national curses.

CHAPTER NINE

What About the Sin of the Jews?
A Broken People

So the angel who talked with me said to me, 'Cry out, thus says the Lord of hosts: I am exceedingly jealous for Jerusalem and for Zion. And I am exceedingly angry with the nations that are at ease; for while I was angry but a little, they furthered the disaster.'

ZECHARIAH 1:14–15 ESV

THIS CHAPTER IS WRITTEN FOR THOSE WELL-MEANING CHRISTIANS who may even agree partially with the message of this book. Nevertheless, they often comment and ask questions similar to these: What about the sin of the Jews? What about Jews like George Soros, Jeffrey Epstein, Albert Einstein, the Rothschilds, *sonderkommandos, kapos,*[5] and the

---

5   *Sondercommandos* were work units in the Nazi death camps with mainly Jewish prisoners forced to work in and around the crematoria. *Kapos* were Nazi death camp prisoners assigned to supervise other prisoners.

millions of Jews who have rejected Jesus Christ? What about the sins of those Jews who actually murdered Him? What about Jews who hate the State of Israel, such as the Neturei Karta[6], who have met with Iranian leaders to show support for their aim of annihilating Israel? Also, look at those Jews who are pro-Palestinian and anti-Zionist today: aren't they like some Jews in the past who have even sold out other Jews (e.g., the Nazis) for money or survival? What about those Jews who hate Christians?

Why don't you ask the Jews to repent, Archbishop, and make restitution to the World?

> "Why cry about your fracture? Your pain has no cure. Because your iniquity is vast, your sins innumerable, I did these things to you. Yet all who devour you will be devoured, and all your foes—all of them—will go into captivity. Those plundering you will be plundered, and all preying on you I give as prey. For I will restore health to you and will heal you of your wounds." It is a declaration of Adonai. "For they called you an outcast: 'Zion—no one cares about her.'"
>
> Jeremiah 30:15–17

The Jewish people are a deeply broken people, a nation of overcomers and survivors who are still recovering from 2,000 years of incredibly tragic history. The story of my family alone is extremely revealing. But, if we research deeply, we will find

---

6   An international ultra-Orthodox Jewish anti-Zionist group

that most Jewish families have a terrible, tragic story. We just do not talk about it.

We are the product of parental demonization. It is in the same way that my son, who passed away at age 35, was a product of parental demonization, which caused terrible self-hatred. His paternal family demonized me to him, and my Messiah was demonized to him as well. This left him terribly broken.

The Jewish people of today are a product of nearly 1,800 years of parental demonization. Let me explain:

In a torn family, when one parent demonizes the other parent, it is parental demonization. Children cannot cope with that. It affects their identity, and it causes self-hatred that could lead to murder or suicide. For nearly 1,800 years, Christians who did not know any better demonized Father God to the Jews. They conveyed to them that their God had forsaken them forever, that they were unredeemable, and that they deserved to be humiliated, plundered, and murdered. They called them subhumans, an accursed race, rats, and vermin. Even today, some Jews going to school or synagogue are tackled by bullies who hurt them and hurl insults at them for "murdering Christ." I have been a witness of this even in twenty-first-century America and as far away as Australia. Most of the Jews I know have similar stories.

This one deception "Jews killed Jesus Christ, so they deserve to die" has led to the murder of more Jews than any other. To make it clear, those who killed the Messiah were not "the Jews" but the Romans instigated by a mob hired by the apostate high priest of the time. The Jews had no jurisdiction under Roman occupation to execute the death penalty. Thousands of Jews followed Yeshua across Israel, and there was a great revival, even among the priesthood. Secondly, Yeshua, the Jewish Messiah, was not murdered. He was a willing sacrifice[7], and only a willing sacrifice can atone for the sin of both Jews and Gentiles alike.

Thus, on top of demonizing God to us, we have been demonized by all other people, as Israel is demonized by the UN nearly every day, unfairly and unjustly. And the people of Israel are the mother of the nations. Without Israel, there is no Bible, no moral code or compass, no Messiah, no gospel!

> Yet all who devour you will be devoured, and all
> your foes—all of them— will go into captivity.
> Those plundering you will be plundered, and all
> preying on you I give as prey.
>
> Jeremiah 30:16

Has Yah punished the people of Israel for sinning against Him? Yes, He has. He exiled us for 2,000 years, but now He has returned us to the land. He does not seek to destroy us but to restore us. The nations are called to comfort the Jewish people, not to confront us.

> "Comfort, comfort My people," says your God.
> Speak kindly to the heart of Jerusalem and proclaim
> to her that her warfare has ended, that her iniquity

---

[7]   John 10:17-18, 1 John 3:16, 1 Tim. 2:6

has been removed. For she has received from Adonai's hand double for all her sins."

Isaiah 40:1–2

We have received double for all our sins, and people are still seeking to punish us? This does not sit right with the God of Israel. Anyone who opposes this restoration because of religious arrogance and hatred against Jews is in grave danger of serious judgment!

> "and I am infuriated with the haughty nations. I was a little angry with them, but they furthered their own calamity. Therefore," thus says Adonai, "I will return to Jerusalem with compassion. My House will be built there," declares Adonai–Tzva'ot "and a measuring line will be stretched out over Jerusalem." Again cry out, saying, thus says Adonai–Tzva'ot, "My cities will again overflow with prosperity and Adonai will again comfort Zion and will again choose Jerusalem."

> Zechariah 1:15–17

The sins of the Jews are not the Gentiles' business, in the same way that the sin of the Gibeonites was none of David's business. Though they lied to Joshua, David needed to make restitution for his predecessor's sin.

> Now there was a famine in the days of David for three years, year after year, so David sought the face of Adonai. Adonai replied, "It is because of Saul

and his bloody house, for he put the Gibeonites to death."

2 Samuel 21:1

In the same manner, the sin of Noah, when he got drunk and was naked in his tent, was none of Ham's business. Noah was his father, and Israel is the mother of the nations. Noah cursed Ham and his seed, Canaan.

> When Noah woke up from his wine, he learned what his youngest son had done to him. So he said, "Cursed is Canaan: the lowest slave will he be to his brothers."

Genesis 9:24–25

Yet he blessed Shem and Japheth, who covered and protected his name.

> He also said, "Blessed be Adonai, God of Shem, and let Canaan be his servant. May God enlarge Japheth, may he dwell in the tents of Shem, and may Canaan be his slave."

Genesis 9:26–27

Later on, YHVH would command the Israelites to destroy all the Canaanites, the descendants of Ham. Slavery also became the outcome of the curse of Ham.

The only thing to do when we see the sin of our parents is to stand in the gap for them and ask for mercy. And if you have sinned against your parents, you must ask forgiveness and make restitution.

Honoring parents is a commandment that carries a promise. This does not depend on your parents' condition.

> "Honor your father and your mother just as Adonai your God commanded you, so that your days may be long, and it may go well with you in the land Adonai your God is giving you."
>
> Deuteronomy 5:16

The Key of Abraham in Genesis 12:3 is based upon that principle of honoring parents. Remember: Israel is the mother of the nations!

> I will bless those who bless you and those who dishonor you I will curse.
>
> Genesis 12:3

We do not sanction the sins of parents, but we are careful not to sin by judging or punishing them.

YHVH punished His people Israel, and the Gentile Christians fell into the sin of Ham and much, much worse. The wicked deeds of Christianity and Christians against the Jews are too many and too wicked to count. Thus, YHVH wants to destroy all nations because of it.

> So the angel who talked with me said to me, "Cry out, Thus says the Lord of hosts: I am exceedingly jealous for Jerusalem and for Zion. And I am exceedingly angry with the nations that are at ease;

for while I was angry but a little, they furthered the disaster."

Zechariah 1:14–15 ESV

For Adonai is enraged at all the nations, and furious at all their armies. He will utterly destroy them. He will give them over to slaughter. For Adonai has a day of vengeance, a year of recompense for the hostility against Zion.

Isaiah 34:2, 8

Only acts of restitution can stop this prophesied destruction! All the most devastating antisemitic events, all the way to the Nazi Shoah (Holocaust), happened in the name of Jesus Christ. We must expose, confront, and repent of them. We cannot cover them up any longer, for it is time that Christian nations and individuals humble themselves and make restitution.

The voice of these ashes is crying for vengeance, and judgment must begin in the house of God, in the church.

"For the time has come for judgment to begin with the house of God. If judgment begins with us first, what will be the end for those who disobey the good news of God?"

1 Peter 4:17

The Jewish people of today bear the wounds of devastating cruelty from the hands of those in mostly Christian nations. Their acts of cruelty, humiliation, plunder, and genocidal murder have left the Jews as broken people. And though we have risen out of the ashes of this cruel hatred to establish the only democracy in the Middle East and have become contributing citizens in every society, Christianity has left us broken. The restoration of the Jewish nation is all that the Almighty cares about. His main goal is to restore His people until they can believe in Him. The Gentile Christians have demonized the Father in heaven to them by misrepresenting the Messiah as a Roman Christ who hates them and their Jewishness. This is parental demonization, and the ravage of this has left people broken for generations. The glory of YHVH will be poured out on those who repent of antisemitism and dedicate themselves to comforting the Jewish people, upon those who make restitution for past and present sins committed by many church denominations against the Jews and the State of Israel.

"Comfort, comfort My people," says your God. "Speak kindly to the heart of Jerusalem and proclaim to her that her warfare has ended, that her iniquity has been removed. For she has received from Adonai's hand double for all her sins." A voice cries out in the wilderness, "Prepare the way of Adonai, make straight in the desert a highway for our God. Every valley will be lifted up, every mountain and hill made low, the rough ground will be a plain and the rugged terrain smooth. The glory of Adonai will be revealed, and all flesh will see it together. For the mouth of Adonai has spoken."

Isaiah 40:1–5

CHAPTER TEN

On Biblical Restitution

WHEN WE REPENT OF OUR SINS (SIN: THE breaking of Yah's [God's] commandments), we are released from the judgment and the penalty we deserve. Yeshua, our Jewish Messiah and Savior, paid with His blood for us to be forgiven and set free from eternal judgment. Our sins towards YHVH God were fully paid on the cross. But the consequences of sinning against man do not disappear when we give our hearts to Messiah; it is these that demand restitution.

Whenever we wrong someone, we must do our best to make it right. Whenever we have a debt, we need to do our best to repay it. A murderer who repents and receives forgiveness from God based on the Messiah's sacrifice may still have to serve a life sentence or even be executed for his crime against humanity. An adulterer who repents and receives eternal life through Yeshua's blood sacrifice may still lose their spouse and their children.

The generations of the Nazis, any Christian, or Christian and Muslim nations who hated, tortured and humiliated, spoiled, and murdered the Jewish people at any time throughout history will still suffer the consequences up to ten generations and forever if no restitution is made.

> No Ammonite or Moabite may enter the assembly of YHVH. Even to the tenth generation, none of them may enter the assembly of YHVH forever, because they did not meet you with bread and with water on the way, when you came out of Egypt, and because they hired against you Balaam the son of Beor from Pethor of Mesopotamia, to curse you. But YHVH your God would not listen to Balaam; instead YHVH your God turned the curse into a blessing for you, because YHVH your God loved you. You shall not seek their peace or their prosperity all your days forever.
>
> Deuteronomy 23:3–6 STB

This may be the case, especially if there is no repentance for the sin of antisemitism against both the God of Israel and the Jewish people. Repentance for sins committed against God allows us to receive the atonement provided by the shed blood of the Jewish Messiah, leading to the salvation of the soul. Repentance for sins committed against men needs to be followed by acts of restitution. Such was the case with King David. David was suffering for the sins of Saul, his predecessor, though he was not to blame for them.

> Now there was a famine in the days of David for three years, year after year, so David sought the face of Adonai. Adonai replied, "It is because of Saul and his bloody house, for he put the Gibeonites to death."
>
> 2 Samuel 21:1

In the same way, many Christians and Christian nations are suffering today for sins committed throughout history against the Jews in the name of Christianity. David knew that the only way out of this curse was to make restitution that would satisfy the Gibeonites.

> David asked the Gibeonites, "What should I do for you? How may I make atonement so that you would bless the inheritance of Adonai?"
>
> 2 Samuel 21:3

The blessing of the Gibeonites was needed for the curse to be broken. The act of restitution was needed to satisfy the Gibeonites so that they would bless David and his Israelite kingdom. The blessing of the Jews from families that suffered during the Nazi Shoah, the pogroms in Russia, the mass murders in Ukraine, the Spanish Inquisition, and more, is needed by the Christians. The judgment of God on this matter has already started. The world is shaking; the earthquakes and storms are more devastating, the wars and the famines have deepened, the plagues are more threatening, recessions are lurking everywhere, and totalitarian regimes are on the threshold of many countries that are suffering from unrest. The most alarming thing in the midst of this shaking are the antisemitic winds blowing all over America and the world.

> For thus says Adonai-Tzva'ot, "He has sent me after glory to the nations that plundered you—because whoever touches you touches the apple of His eye—"
>
> Zechariah 2:8 (Hebrews: v. 12)

> For Adonai has a day of vengeance, a year of recompense for the hostility against Zion.
>
> Isaiah 34:8

The blessing of the people of Israel is needed by the nations of the world that perpetrated the crimes, were accomplices, or did nothing to stop them. This includes most of Christendom; Catholics, Protestants, and Evangelicals. Only true humility like King David's, coupled with acts of restitution, can overturn this curse on humanity. Doing the right thing before God is always a personal protection in times of judgment.

> "If I shut up heaven that there is no rain, or if I command the locust to devour the land, or if I send pestilence among My people, when My people, over whom My Name is called, humble themselves and pray and seek My face and turn from their evil ways, then I will hear from heaven and will forgive their sin and will heal their land."
>
> 2 Chronicles 7:13–14

When I was saved out of my own sins and terrible family tragedy, my business collapsed, and I had many debts. I broke my retirement pension fund and paid them. Later on, I went to work and paid for the rest of the bounced checks. Faith in Yeshua did not exempt me from paying. That faith propelled me to do what was right and to pay my debts. And as long as I seek to do what is right, He is there to help me, and His grace is sufficient for me.

The blood of Yeshua wipes our slate clean with Yah, but not with man. This is the key to understanding the need for restitution towards the Jewish people, the people of Israel of today.

Before meeting Messiah at the age of twenty-eight and my ensuing repentance, I had committed adultery. My first husband suffered from bipolar disorder and made my life a misery. I fell prey to desperation and anger, then to the arms of another to receive some love and comfort. I fell into the hands of Satan, the ouija board, and the occult to find answers for my crumbling life and for my husband's mental illness. My baby son was then ten months old, and my daughter was four years old. Even though I repented before God and was gloriously saved by Yeshua, the consequences of my previous sin toward my family have been a big part of the suffering of my life.

Though there were many extenuating circumstances that led me to sin, I did my best to make restitution right after my salvation. By then, the father of my children had divorced me. I offered to serve him and the children as a mere maid or housekeeper until the children reached the age of eighteen and would be considered adults by Israeli law. I was willing to give up all my rights or plans for almost seventeen years until my son was eighteen. I did not demand conjugal rights; I was willing to be a maid. My ex-husband refused my offer on account of my faith in Messiah Yeshua. However, it was that faith that led me to offer such radical restitution. His refusal to forgive or receive restitution of any kind took the whole case out of my hands and enabled me to proceed on my journey with Yeshua. This released me to marry for the first time in Messiah, leading me to preach the gospel in over fifty nations. My conscience is clean in this matter because I tried my best; the rest I left in the hands of my God.

Restitution is not a one-time deal; sometimes, it is a lifelong exercise, as it was for Shaul (Paul), the Jewish apostle to the Gentiles. He lived a life of restitution for persecuting and murdering the community of Messianic believers in Yeshua.

> **"For I will show him how much he must suffer for the sake of My Name."**
>
> **Acts 9:16 ESV**

When we do what is right toward humanity and make restitution for wronging humanity, it is for His name's sake that we are suffering. Doing the right thing for people honors Yeshua.

Paul was so stricken for having formerly persecuted and murdered the Jewish believers that he was willing to pay with his eternal life for their salvation. It shows the extent and depth of his repentance, by which acts of restitution must always follow.

I tell the truth in Messiah—I do not lie, my conscience assuring me in the Ruach ha-Kodesh (Holy Spirit)—that my sorrow is great and the anguish in my heart unending. For I would pray that I myself were cursed, banished from Messiah for the sake of my people—my own flesh and blood.

Romans 9:1–3

The one who wanted His Jewish people (those that believed in Messiah) dead, was now willing to die, even eternally, for them to be saved! That is the heart of true restitution.

This must be our heart as well, every believer in every nation. We must hear the voice of the Father regarding His beloved chosen people and their holy land, taking action for repentance and restitution as He clearly leads. The harvest of many souls depends upon our obedience as end time events unfold, challenging us to go beyond what we may currently understand. Let us recall the words of the mother of Yeshua, which set the stage for water to turn to wine at the wedding in Cana: "Whatever He says to you, do it." (John 2:5) Simple obedience has the potential to produce miracles!

PRAYER OF REPENTANCE

Father in Heaven, thank You for the Truth contained in the pages of this book that makes me free. I choose to humble my heart to let You in. I ask Your forgiveness for myself, my family, my church, my city, my land, and my nation for all the sins of commission and omission against Israel and the Jewish People, Your People, for taking them lightly and dishonoring them in any way.

I ask Your forgiveness for all antisemitism in religious doctrine, thought, word, or deed and for my ignorance and our ignorance about this important subject of restitution. I reject all anti-Jewish and anti-Israel sentiments I or my generations have had against Your People, knowingly or unknowingly. I ask You to help, lead, and teach me to walk this Road of Restitution that will bring freedom and revival to my life, family, church community, and nation in Yeshua, the Jewish Messiah's name whom I embrace as my Savior, Lord, and King. Amen.

MY PRAYER FOR YOU

I extend my forgiveness as a Jew to you and your people for the sins committed against my People, the Jews, the People of Israel.

I break the curses that have fallen upon you, your generations, and your nation because of any manner of antisemitism in doctrine or deed, and I bless you to walk and thrive as you put the principles of Restitution outlined in this book into action and teach others to do the same. In Yeshua's name. Amen.

The Key of Abraham opens or closes the door to the blessing or the curse to all peoples and nations.

My desire is to bless those who bless you (Jewish
People, Israel) but whoever curses you I will curse,
and in you all the families of the earth will be blessed.

Genesis 12:3 TLV

The following chapters contain the stories of three faithful
leaders in our ministry. The Spirit of Yah spoke to them about
the importance of restitution towards the Jewish people. Each
one comes from a different Christian background, and I did
not expressly teach them what you will read in the following
few chapters. Their testimonies and revelation have propelled
me to write this book. I realized that this divine call to make
restitution for Christian antisemitism leading to the Nazi
Shoah is an end-time move of the Holy Spirit. I invite you to
hear their voices.

CHAPTER ELEVEN

Pastor Cesar Silva of Mexico: Restoring Honor to Israel

I CAME TO REALIZE THAT RESTORING ISRAEL'S HONOR was as urgent as it was necessary for the healing of my city, nation, life, and family. I understood that there was no longer time to remain bankrupt spiritually, physically, financially, and emotionally, because it all leads to the same thing: emptiness and destruction.

This process to restore honor begins with the wonderful teachings we have received from the ministry of the Apostle Dominiquae Bierman, who, through the revelation of the powerful Key of Abraham (Gen 12:3, which opens the doors), sowed within my heart that seed that is now bearing fruit in and around my life.

A day came when the Ruach (Spirit of Elohim) gave me a dream. In the dream, I saw that I had left my vehicle at a primary entrance of the city of Rio Bravo (where I live), and along that avenue came a river of blood due to deaths caused by the drug trade. I saw that the river was almost reaching us. I quickly went to my vehicle because I knew that inside of it was the offering that the church had given to be sent to Israel. I knew that this offering would provide restitution and would cause a diminishing of that river of blood. The Ruach HaKodesh was also telling me that, indeed, this would stop this river of blood. Thus, I opened the truck and, thanks be to the Lord, the money was still there!

In northern Mexico, there is a constant war between drug cartels and the armed forces. There is a continual danger of finding oneself in the middle of a firearms confrontation. That is why the Ruach told me through this dream that we must restore honor to Israel through offerings, along with prayer and humbling ourselves to repent for the hatred of Israel by the nations of the earth. This strategy brings freedom from death and the river of blood. This will make a difference because the powerful Key of Abraham is put into action; it is the key to prayers being answered and mercy being poured out instead of anger.

After dreaming this, we spoke and prayed and blessed Israel with genuine actions and offerings. As a consequence, we saw our prayers for protection of our city answered, and I felt an atmosphere of peace. It diminished the criminal activity of the cartels.

RESTORE HONOR—IT'S A COMMANDMENT OF THE TORAH!

Then the Lord spoke to Moses, saying, "When a person sins and acts unfaithfully against the Lord, and deceives his companion in regard to a deposit or a security entrusted to him, or through robbery, or if he has extorted from his companion, or has found what was lost and lied about it and sworn falsely, so that he sins in regard to any one of the things a man may do; then it shall be, when he sins and becomes guilty, that he shall restore what he took by robbery or what he got by extortion, or the deposit which was entrusted to him or the lost thing which he found, or anything about which he swore falsely; he shall make restitution for it in full and add to it one-fifth more. He shall give it to the one to whom it belongs on the day he presents his guilt offering. Then he shall bring to the priest his guilt offering to the Lord, a ram without defect from the flock, according to your valuation, for a guilt offering, and the priest shall make atonement for him before the Lord, and he will be forgiven for any one of the things which he may have done to incur guilt."

Leviticus 6:1–7 NASB

Just as we desire to be made whole when someone offends us, steals from us, or slanders us, so we, the nations of the world, need to realize how we are indebted to the blessed people of Israel. The promise of Genesis 12:3 still stands, "I will bless those who bless you and the one who curses you I will curse."

The Global Re-Education Initiative (GRI) Against Anti-Semitism,[8] led by Apostle Dominiquae Bierman, is not only necessary but urgent! The sick who will die shall be numbered in millions amidst plagues that will scourge the earth without end, unless the Lord finds someone who fully understands what it is to restore honor to Israel. Restitution is more than asking for forgiveness! Truly, asking for forgiveness is the first thing we must do when we know we have done wrong, but *to restore honor to someone*, we must do more than just apologize.

In history, we find that when a man was questioned about his honor, an appointment was made to settle the dispute, and he said, "I challenge to a duel the knight who has questioned my honor." Then people knew that the person who came to defend his honor considered it greater than all the slander against him.

We, the nations of the world, have committed a great dishonor by using slanderous and lying words against Israel, staining her honor. So, it is time to repent, ask for forgiveness, and restore her honor. In Leviticus 6:5, when an offering was made for the guilt of slander, the person acknowledged the damage and asked for forgiveness with his atonement offering to the Lord. Afterward, it was time to *restore*, as it is written:

---

[8]   www.Against-Antisemitism.com

> ... he shall make restitution for it in full and add to it
> one-fifth more; he shall give it to the one who belongs
> to him on the day he presents his guilt offering.
>
> Leviticus 6:5

In Leviticus 6:6, God adds that the offering should be given to the priest.

> Then he shall bring to the priest his guilt offering
> to the Lord.
>
> Leviticus 6:6 NASB

Besides repenting, making restitution for the damage, and adding the fifth part (20%), it was necessary to give it to the priest; so, we must present it to the minister who can pray for us in order that we may receive mercy from the Eternal. Do you know who has ready access to ask Adonai to have mercy on us? Yes, the answer is the Jewish people of today. They are His chosen ones, the light of the nations. They are our priests who will open the way for Adonai to forgive us and for the refreshing of His presence to come (Acts 3:19).

The Hebrew words *shuv* and *shalem* clarify the concept of restitution. The word "will restitute" (Lev 6:4) is the Hebrew word *shuv*, from which we derive the word *teshuvah*, meaning "turn or return" or "repentance for a great restoration." And the word "restore" in Leviticus 6:5 is the word *shalam*, which means here "to make payment," coming from the word *leshalem*, which means "to make a payment." So, to make peace, you need to make *a payment of restitution*. Yeshua mentioned this in Matthew chapter 5.

"You have heard that the ancients were told, 'You shall not commit murder' and 'Whoever commits murder shall be liable to the court.' But I say to you that everyone who is angry with his brother shall be guilty before the court; and whoever says to his brother, 'You good-for-nothing,' shall be guilty before the supreme court; and whoever says, 'You fool,' shall be guilty enough to go into the fiery hell. Therefore, if you are presenting your offering at the altar, and there remember that your brother has something against you, leave your offering there before the altar and go; first be reconciled to your brother, and then come and present your offering. Make friends quickly with your opponent at law while you are with him on the way, so that your opponent may not hand you over to the judge, and the judge to the officer, and you be thrown into prison. Truly, I say to you, you will not come out of there until you have paid up the last cent."

Matthew 5:21–26

This Scripture passage speaks about the power of restitution, but let's go a little deeper into how anti-Judaism works. Because of antisemitism, there have been murders, hatred, and armies against the Jewish people. Much of this hatred is under the mask of Christianity, which claims to give Sunday offerings to God. But my question is this: will the Eternal YHVH of Israel look with favor upon those offerings, which with one hand are offered to Him, while the other hand holds a knife of hate, anger, and even a death wish against the people of Israel? The answer is simple; He is not receiving those offerings! Thus, Yeshua's advice is to reconcile with your brother Judah first and make peace. So, restore and make peace.

THIS IS ALL ABOUT RESTORING HONOR TO ISRAEL

In every kingdom, we know that the king's eldest son is the crown prince; he will one day become king. This is true in any of the kingdoms we still know, and it is very interesting that YHVH is the king and that he called one of Abraham's descendants "My first-born" (Exod 4:22). The one known as "My prince" was originally called Jacob. Still, Adonai decided that his name would be known as Israel, meaning "Prince of Elohim." What a substantial difference! But what a stark contrast to how the nations of the world refer to Israel; they say Israel is just one more nation on earth, like any other nation. In the eyes of the living Elohim, however, they are not just any nation; they are "His prince."

Today I hear many people talking about the kingdom of God: the manifestation of the kingdom of God, how they seek the kingdom of God, and about their job being to extend the kingdom of YHVH. But they stumble over this principle. That's why they're on a treadmill like hamsters, just words and more words without results and we do not see the establishment of the kingdom of YHVH. Why? Because they stumble on the stone of stumbling, but he who believes the word of Elohim shall love and embrace this prince, which is Israel. For them it will be "like the shade of a huge rock in a parched land" (Isa 32:2), while he who takes it lightly "will be broken to pieces ... scattered like dust" (Matt 21:44).

CONCLUSION

The nations of the world are indebted to the people of Israel, for they gave us the Torah, the covenants, the promises, the revelation of the living Elohim, and Yeshua HaMashiach ('the Messiah' in Hebrew). Today we must turn completely to *Him*, loving His Torah (which is Yeshua incarnate), and restoring honor to Israel, the prince of God. I am a witness of His goodness, for surely the Lord means what He says.

I will bless those who bless you, and the one who curses you, I will curse.

Genesis 12:3

Pastor César Silva, Rio Bravo, Tamaulipas, México
UNIFY[9] National Delegate for Mexico

CHAPTER TWELVE

Pastor Perach Yang of Taiwan: Revelations on Restitution

In May 2021 during the COVID-19 pandemic, Taiwan experienced a severe drought that led to depleted reservoirs. We understood that we needed to repent and make a restitution offering together. Thus, we united in prayer, beginning by repenting of the sin of Anti-MESITOJUZ[10] and, following 2 Chronicles 7:14, we made a restitution offering to Israel for the healing of our land.

> If My people who are called by My Name will humble themselves, and pray and seek My face, and turn from their wicked ways, then I will hear from heaven, and I will forgive their sin and will heal their land.

> 2 Chronicles 7:14

---

[10]   Anti-Messiah, Anti-Israel, Anti-Torah, Anti-Jewish, Anti-Zionism. For more information about the subject, order *The Identity Theft* at www. Against-Antisemitism.com

The following day, during Shabbat, I heard a whisper saying the word "ten." It immediately brought to mind Genesis 18:22–23, 32, where Abraham asked God to spare Sodom and Gomorrah from destruction, but a minimum of ten righteous people would be required to stand in the gap for those cities.

On Shavuot 2022, our Taiwan UNIFY team repented on behalf of our government and people for the sin of Anti-MESITOJUZ, sending again a restitution offering to UNIFY. There were exactly ten of us: a few GRM Bible School[11] graduates, students, and others who had been immersed in the name of Yeshua. Two aboriginal couples joined us as well. Miraculously, a wonderful rain extinguished an eight-day forest fire on Taiwan's tallest peak that afternoon and continued to fall the next day. How profoundly grateful we were to Abba for answering our prayer!

Pastor Tsai, a long-time preacher of Jewish roots in Taiwan, also joined us in our repentance act, and she continued to preach the importance of making restitution to Israel and the Jewish people. She gathered fifty-one individuals to repent on behalf of Taiwan's government and its people for the sin of Anti-MESITOJUZ and, as a result, abundant rain replenished Taiwan's reservoirs, ending the drought!

JEWISH SOULS SET FREE

During an online Shabbat prayer session, we repented for the mistreatment of Jews, as described in *The Healing Power of the Roots.*[12] Amidst our prayers, I had a vision:

---

11   GRM Israeli Bible Institute: www.GRMBibleInstitute.com

12   Available at www.ZionsGospel.com

Tens of thousands of Jews, dressed in black and white Nazi camp prisoner attire, steadily emerged from what appeared to be a concentration/death camp, walking towards a vast road.

As I watched the vision, tears fell down my face. Could it be that when we repented and made a restitution offering to UNIFY on behalf of the church, not only did we receive God's forgiveness, but also these souls of (murdered) Jews were set free? We then fervently prayed for the salvation of their living Jewish descendants, aligning with Archbishop Dominiquae's vow in Auschwitz: "For every drop of blood, for every ash of exterminated Jews I demand that a soul be saved."*

Then, during the annual Sukkot Israel tour in Jerusalem, we held a ceremony to rededicate the delegates and vice-delegates of the United Nations for Israel. Following the proclamation of the UNIFY manifesto[13] and receiving the rabbi's Aaronic blessing, I experienced another vision:

The railway tracks at Auschwitz death camp were illuminated, with light emanating from within the camp, towards the outside.

These two visions conveyed a unified message from Yah: The Lord has not forgotten the tragic fate of His covenant people. Furthermore, the declaration made by the UNIFY delegates holds profound significance that, through repentance and making restitution for the sins of bloodshed on earth, we can bring comfort to Jewish souls and prevent the cries of innocent blood from echoing out of the ground any longer (Gen 4:10).

The Lord also led me to understand that while living under the threat of war from China, we need more people to study

---

[13]   www.unitednationsforisrael.org/manifesto/

the GRM Bible school, to be cleansed from the deception and lies of replacement theology, and to repent and make restitution to the Jews. Replacement theology is the beginning of the separation of the Jewish Messiah and His Jewish people from the Gentile believers, and it started the demonization of the Jews that has continued until today.

By joining and agreeing with UNIFY, as I declared the UNIFY manifesto, I saw that the souls in the death camps were comforted and set free, and the Auschwitz death camp will no longer be buried in death, but will have light and life, both for Jews and Gentiles. Thus, the Holy Spirit revealed that acts of restitution—prayer and offerings to UNIFY—bring comfort and rest to the Jewish blood crying out from the ground. UNIFY's actions are affecting Jewish souls through acts of restitution. The curse is being overturned to become a blessing!

This is at the heart of everything we do at UNIFY.

THE WINDOW OF MERCY

Again, another vision came to me:

A large, white, shining hand has lifted a door/window frame from "the ground." When this frame was erected, it was filled with a great light and a flowing anointing that went deep and far and was glorious.

A few minutes after the vision appeared, I read Archbishop Dominiquae's article *My Journey* that tells about her visit to Auschwitz where God called her to be the voice of these ashes. I was very moved by it, but I did not really understand the meaning of "the window of mercy" mentioned in the article. But, after the act of repentance and restitution that ended the drought in Taiwan, I understood that "the window of mercy" was indeed opened for the "restoration of the land." May you too find this window of mercy by doing the right thing by standing in the gap in repentance and restitution for your nation.

> The window of mercy has been opened for a very short time, and the United Nations for Israel is the platform that He has given to us in order to release that mercy. It is based on repentance and acts of restitution towards Israel and the Jewish people. The blessing or the curse upon individuals and entire nations depends on this! Forgiveness is free, but it's not cheap; it requires action![14]

Pastor Perach Yang,
UNIFY Delegate for Taiwan

---

[14]   www.unitednationsforisrael.org/my-journey/

CHAPTER THIRTEEN

Apostle Sana Enroos of Sweden: Acts of Restitution

OUR UNDERSTANDING OF RESTITUTION TOWARDS THE JEWISH PEOPLE has not been adequate because of replacement theology and its countless lies about the Jews. Sins committed in the name of Christianity and Jesus Christ against the Jewish people are brutal. The blood of the murdered Jews is crying out from the ground for vengeance, like Abel's blood did after Cain murdered his brother (Gen 4:10). We are in debt to the Jewish people for so many things: They gave us the Torah, the Messiah and, through Him, our salvation. Salvation is from the Jews (John 4:22). We have not always been grateful because of misunderstandings. Yah calls us to restore the honor of the Jewish people by blessing them with our righteous actions. Israel is our mother!

Honor your father and your mother, so that your days may be long upon the land which Adonai your

God is giving you.

Exodus 20:12

Acts of repentance are deeply needed for the sins that we as Christians have committed. We have taken Israel and the Jews lightly, and these sins of a nation against the Jewish people require acts of repentance that should always be followed by making restitution. This is how we can use the Key of Abraham (Gen 12:3) on behalf of our families, generations, and nations.

And I will bless those who bless you, and the one who curses you I will curse. And in you all the families of the earth will be blessed.

Genesis 12:3 NASB

Years ago, I received a calling to do things for the Jews in Sweden that nobody had ever done before. These acts of repentance and restitution raise the shield of honor over the Jewish people, and what we do to them, we do to Yeshua Himself:

And answering, the King will say to them, 'Amen, I tell you, whatever you did to one of the least of these My brethren, you did it to Me.'

Matthew 25:40

This also releases blessings to us and our nation. Every time I need wisdom, a solution, or a breakthrough, I unlock the Key of Abraham by seeking ways to bless the Jews according to the word "to the Jew first." (Rom 1:16). Below I am sharing with you some examples of what kind of acts have been done to provide restitution towards the Jewish people and Israel through United Nations for Israel in Sweden and Scandinavia.

CLEANING JEWISH CEMETERIES

In Sweden, we have done much cleaning at the Jewish cemeteries. There are 8,800 graves in Stockholm's active Jewish cemeteries, and I have been led to them, again and again, to clean the gravestones, ridding them of rubbish, fallen branches, and old candles. I have felt such joy in doing this!

You may ask how this would help anyone to be saved or if there is any purpose in cleaning a Jewish cemetery. Ruach, the Holy Spirit, gave us this initiative showing that it is an act of restitution towards the Jewish people by Sweden, which has taken Israel lightly and persecuted the Jews.

One day, I was cleaning the Northern Jewish Cemetery. It was a beautiful morning, and I felt expectancy in the atmosphere. I was picking up fallen dead branches, garbage, and old flowers, and cleaning the moss and lichen from the gravestones. As I continued my work, a new song was born in my spirit in Finnish. Its simple lyrics were based on Romans 1:16 and Genesis 12:3: *"Always to the Jews first, so that a nation would be blessed."* I felt that this cleaning prepared the way in the Spirit for our special prayer mission against Nazism in Stockholm. It was the right thing to do before proceeding forward.

During the summer of 2022, Ruach led me to clean the Jewish cemeteries seven times. "You are unlocking your heavenly blessings by doing this," He spoke clearly into my heart. I understood that even if my sole purpose was only to honor the Jews, He would not deny blessings that follow every time we use the key of Abraham (Gen 12:3).

Once, when I asked Abba what He thought about cleaning the Jewish graves, Yeshua's answer blew me away: "Cleaning one Jewish grave is like tying My sandals." I was amazed and moved, sighing, "What an honor, Yeshua!" I understood that He would do the same for the least of His brethren, and walking in precise obedience is walking in Yeshua's footsteps.

Cleaning Jewish cemeteries has been established as an act of honor towards the Jewish people in Sweden. I have done this in Stockholm, and other team members have cleaned the cemeteries and honored the Jewish graves with white marble stones in Sundsvall, Norrköping, Gothenburg, and Malmö. Every time we have done this, we feel refreshed, blessed, and filled with deep shalom. It touches our Father's heart and pleases Him as we practice the principle "To the Jews first." Personal blessings and breakthroughs have been released after these missions, especially regarding wisdom and finances.

LIGHT MISSIONS

Hanukkah Lights 2021 in Sweden

Obedience in one area leads you to the next level in your faith. When you act for the Jewish people, even in secret, Yah sees and rewards you. He will not let it go unnoticed. While cleaning the Jewish cemetery in November 2021, the Holy Spirit gave me a mission for Hanukkah: Lighting 1,200 candles on the graves in the Northern Jewish Cemetery in Stockholm. For ten hours, we worked hard with a small team to light all 1,200 candles on the graves. The purpose was to honor and bless the Jews. This was also an act of restitution for the sins of Christianity. We proclaimed that we would remember the names of these Jews and honor their memories; if their names are forgotten, nobody will remember anymore.

It was a very moving and beautiful work, and our Father was so pleased. Ruach showed me that this was historical and would not go unnoticed by heaven and earth. This impacted the whole nation! Two days after the mission, I picked up the burned candles in just three hours; angels must have been helping me.

Shoah Remembrance Day, 27 January 2022

I sensed in my spirit that there would be a second candle lighting mission. Indeed, that soon took place in Southern Jewish Cemetery on Shoah Remembrance Day. Yah showed me this would unlock Sweden in the Spirit and get things rolling, and I saw how heaven was especially noticing this act! It was like a key put into a lock and, indeed, the key of Abraham (Gen 12:3) opens all doors!

We were ten righteous ones lighting these candles at the Jewish graves. The purpose was again to honor and bless the Jews, repent for the sins of Christianity, and to remember the names of the deceased and honor their memories. Again, we had 1,200 candles. Now it would be altogether 2,400 candles, symbolizing the twenty-four elders around the throne of Yah. This time, due to heavy wind and rain, it felt like an impossible act. However, we still did it and managed to light all 1,200 candles. Two eagles flew over the cemetery towards the east, crying loudly while we were lighting the candles.

We received from the Holy Spirit the words "Time of *Rachem*, Grace over Sweden." We believe that there will be a shift that will affect congregations and spiritual leaders in our country; those who do not really follow Yeshua and have the right motives will be removed.

An elderly Jewish man passed by and was moved when he saw the star of David built with candles. We told him that we wanted to honor the Jews on Memorial Day and that we believed in Yeshua, and that His true name is not Jesus. The more we talked and the more he asked, the more his eyes filled with tears. This Jewish man had a fear of YHVH when he stood there, and he was very touched. He said that his father had lived through World War II and the Shoah. He returned to us several times, and we continued talking.

Light Mission in Jewish Cemetery in Norway

It was a rainy day, and we were soaked and cold during the first three hours as we were doing another candle-lighting mission, this time in Norway. The last three hours were freezing, but the joy of Adonai gave us strength. It was a struggle to get our 1,000 candles lit at that beautiful small cemetery in Oslo, but then we experienced a breakthrough when the rain stopped.

All the graves and the star of David structure in the middle of the cemetery were filled with candles. It became a memorial for the precious Jewish people. We saw in the spirit how the *magen David* (star of David) burned deep down into the ground and destroyed the Nazi swastika, a familiar sign in Norway and a part of its identity since World War II. Yeshua said, "Everything you do here is preparation for My return." After the act of repentance and prayers, a beautiful shalom was released upon the place, and we felt that the atmosphere in Oslo changed.

SINS OF THE NATION AGAINST ISRAEL AND THE JEWS REQUIRE RESTITUTION

Nations have acted wickedly against the Jewish people, and we need to ask for forgiveness because of these unrighteous acts. All acts of repentance start with personal repentance from replacement theology.

One example of a sin requiring restitution is plundering the Jews by stealing their assets and properties. It is unclear precisely how much gold Sweden obtained during the war; estimates vary from between 20,000 (44,000 lbs) and 34,000 kilos (75,000 lbs). In the early 1950s, some gold was returned to its rightful owners, but declassified archives show that many tons of gold are still unaccounted for.

These gold bars did not originate only from precious metal confiscated from Jews but, in many instances, they had a much more macabre history: they were melted down gold teeth, wedding rings, and golden eyeglass frames taken from Jews in Auschwitz and other death camps. We did an act of repentance because of this plundering of the Jews, especially for all their assets still in Sweden: gold, money, art, valuable objects, literature, etc. After the act of repentance, I felt the curse was broken, and a new financial era would come to Sweden. We also sent a restitution offering to the Jews through United Nations for Israel on behalf of Sweden.

In November 2022, we repented on behalf of the Swedish parliament because Sweden did not vote for Israel in the UN concerning the "occupation" (Judea and Samaria). Norway and Finland remained silent too, and all three countries deserved nothing but *meerah* (a curse in Hebrew) upon them. We sent again a restitution offering to UNIFY on behalf of Sweden, Norway, and Finland.

Giving away books and the GRI Against Anti-Semitism online course of Archbishop Dominiquae can also be seen as restitution towards Jews. The true gospel made in Zion goes forward, and people are reeducated by the truth, coming to love the Jewish people like Ruth loved Naomi. Sacrificial love for Israel will lead you automatically to the acts of restitution. When you receive the gospel of the kingdom that comes through the Jewish Messiah, who Himself came from the Jewish people to whom the land of Israel belongs, you will understand the gift of restitution. It is truly a gift from the Father!

BUILDING MEMORIALS FOR THE JEWISH PEOPLE

In 1992, Sweden refused to allow Jews on their way to Israel to pass through our country, turning 501 Jews back to Russia even if they had been given permission earlier. Sweden became like Edom (Num 20:17–21), and the whole affair brought blood guilt onto the hands of Sweden, and that blood is crying out for vengeance. Those Jews were sent back to Russia and faced difficulties and persecution, and some even perished.

Yah instructed me to build a memorial of stones for the Jews who could not make aliyah through Sweden in 1992. These Jews travelled to Sweden via Estonia. Two years later, on 28 September 1994, the M/S Estonia ferry sailed the same route. It never returned to Stockholm but sank that night. In this tragedy, 501 Swedes died, *the same number* as the Jews who Sweden did not allow to pass through the land. Swedish police officers (63) had been on the ferry, sailing and having fun; none of them were rescued. What a tragedy!

This stone memorial became like an *Ebenezer*, a stone of help, and an act of restitution that would overturn the curse on Sweden. Yah's finger was upon it. I believe that this star of David built with fifty kilos (110 lbs) of white marble stone is an Ebenezer for Sweden, operating for *Rachem*, Mercy! It also became a stone of help for my family because I used the Key of Abraham. When the memorial was finished, heaven was open upon that place. The curse of Edom was broken in Sweden.

Building a Memorial in Finland

There was specific blood guilt in Finland that required action and repentance on behalf of the country. An act of restitution needed to follow the act of repentance for Jews murdered in the Jokela forest. We carried fifty kilos (110 lbs) of white marble stone from Sweden to Finland. This act was carried out in the old, largely forgotten Jewish cemetery, insignificant in appearance and abandoned. The cemetery was last used about 122 years ago when, in 1910, the latest burial occurred. When we saw the gate and the simple wooden star of David, it was like the strongest star of David we had ever seen. We felt that angels were waiting at the gates as guards, saying, "Now they're here for such a time as this."

It is not that these stones themselves carry any significance, but the act of honor does. Prophetic acts of restitution are born for a specific time and place from the Holy Spirit and cannot be copied and made into a formula. Ahvenisto Jewish Cemetery was the strategic place that Yah had chosen to give birth to something new in Finland and erase this blood guilt from the nation. He instructed us to honor that place with a *magen David*, formed from those white marble stones, marking the ground for the gospel made in Zion.

Building a Memorial in Slovakia

Of the 89,000 Jews in Slovakia in 1940, an estimated 69,000 were murdered in the Shoah. The Slovak government organized the transports and paid 500 Reichsmarks per Jew for the supposed cost of resettlement. We repented at the Shoah

Memorial, where I felt deep sorrow for the murdered Jews of Slovakia. All these precious Jewish people exterminated in the genocide flashed before my eyes, and a loud and unstoppable cry came out of my heart! Another Shoah memorial was located at the former Žilina transition camp for the Jews. There was a piece of railway track with the inscription: "Road of no return." We made a *magen David* of 500 white stones as a memorial and an act of honor for the Jewish people. We felt heaven open upon the place, and the city's atmosphere changed.

RESTITUTION BRINGS NATIONAL BREAKTHROUGHS

In the summer of 2022, Yah instructed me to put white stones on all 8,800 Jewish graves in both Jewish cemeteries in Stockholm. It took five days to accomplish this mission with 170 kilos (375 lbs) of white marble stones. All who participated in the missions were blessed above expectations and felt our Father's heart in this. The presence of Yah was strong, and we received great personal encouragement from heaven.

After all these acts of restitution in 2021–2022, Ruach spoke: this land is the platform of revival! This third-day revival will spread throughout Europe, and unlike former revivals, it will never end, and it will not come in the way that many Christians would expect.

After seven acts of restitution towards the Jewish people in Sweden in July, Yah revealed a vast amount of hidden information and revelation regarding antisemitism concerning Sweden and its ungodly connections to Nazi Germany. He also gave us a new mission aimed at blood guilt and Nazism in Sweden and surrounding countries. It became like a hunt for Nazism and antisemitism, to root out the entire evil system.

Our nation has now received a new Israel-friendly government that is a turnaround and the fruit of many acts of repentance and restitution we have done. This is a miracle for which we have been praying for years.

ACTS OF HONOR TOWARDS SHOAH SURVIVORS

Restitution can also be an act of kindness towards the Jewish people and especially towards Shoah (Holocaust) survivors. We named these acts of mercy *Operation Rachem*. Its main purpose is serving and making restitution to the Jewish people in Sweden, especially Shoah survivors and elderly Jews. They are often moved to tears over Operation Rachem and the actions we show them in Yeshua's love; kindness truly opens hearts.

I started to bless a Shoah survivor who survived five death camps by sending him and his wife a loaf of challah bread for Shabbat. They were so grateful. When I told them what we do for the Jewish people, they were amazed, saying: "But this is just fantastic!" Another Shoah survivor said my challah was the best he had ever tasted. Gifts with appreciation have opened their hearts to our Father's love.

A man's gift makes room for him, and leads him before great men.

Proverbs 18:16

One Shoah survivor was saved by Yeshua in his last days. During the last months of his life, he received a lot of love that melted his heart and made him ready to receive Yeshua.

'I was naked and you clothed Me; I was sick and you visited Me; I was in prison and you came to Me.' Then the righteous will answer Him, 'Lord, when did we see You hungry and feed You? Or thirsty and give You something to drink? And when did we see You a stranger and invite You in? Or naked and clothe You? When did we see You sick, or in prison, and come to You?' And answering, the King will say to them, 'Amen, I tell you, whatever you did to one of the least of these My brethren, you did it to Me.'

Matthew 25:36–40

Apostle Sana Enroos, UNIFY Delegate for Sweden
Regional leader of Scandinavia and Europe

CHAPTER FOURTEEN

Testimonies: Power of Restitution

POTENT SEED OF RESTITUTION

During Hanukkah 2022, YHVH asked us to "lend to Him" by giving a special donation for Archbishop's shalom and wellbeing. He prompted us to send this gift to the ministry to support the building of the watchman apartment in Jerusalem. YHVH moved in the hearts of my family and asked us to refinance our house. The bank approved the loan immediately, and we gave the amount during Pesach 2023. When we told Archbishop Dominiquae about this good news, she was already preparing to teach us a message on kingdom wealth. Through this offering, we sowed a seed of restitution for our families and congregation to bless the land of Israel. We took the last smaller batch of the money to Israel to prophetically put it at the Apostle's feet. After the seed was sown, many blessings came forth. The refinanced house has a limit of ninety-nine years on the lease, but shortly afterwards we received news that the court will grant permanent freehold status to the houses in our area! Then my brother Benjamin was promoted and received a 44% salary increase, and my wife's online business received some significant sales volume. Praise Yah!

— Yosef Lo, Malaysia

RELEASE OF COVID RESTRICTIONS

We started a Daniel fast when the COVID-19 outbreak began. A month later, the number of cases rose to 65,000. When we repented on behalf of our nation, the cases dropped to half, and soon the cases were reduced to around 6,000, and government restrictions were partially relaxed for the people with COVID-19. The lion of Judah defeated the dragon. Praise YHVH!

In December 2022, the Ima Bat Ami[15] group in mainland China prayed with our Hong Kong team. During the meeting, Hadassah confessed and repented for Chinese actions, including repentance for the fake nucleic acid tests done by Chinese companies for financial benefit. A few days later, she also repented of antisemitism in China on behalf of herself and her family, and she gave a restitution offering to UNIFY for the purchase of coats for Russian Jewish immigrants in Israel.

A few days later, I saw a news report that indicated that from now on, the health code inspection of cross-regional migrants will no longer be carried out, and the 48-hour nucleic acid negative certificate and health code inspection will no longer be carried out in trains. Patients with asymptomatic infection and mild symptoms could now isolate in homes, and there was

---

[15]   *"Mother daughter of my people."* Our Ima Bat Ami women's prayer & study groups gather in many nations.

also a cancellation of the landing inspection and investigation of the fake nucleic acid testing companies. All glory and power belong to Him!

— Pastor D'vora Cheung, Hong Kong

MENTAL HEALING

I taught about restitution in our Shabbat meeting and received a restitution offering from a person having suicidal thoughts and suffering from mental sickness. She had taken medication for that for more than eight years, and now, after repentance and restitution, she has received healing!

— Pastor Dvora Cheung, Hong Kong

MIRACLES AFTER MIRACLES

We ministered to a lady with cancer and advised her to use the Key of Abraham to activate Adonai's blessing for her life and healing. We instructed her to raise up an offering of restitution that she and her daughter would send to the ministry. After she did that, the situation initially worsened, but it soon turned to victory: the cancer dried up, and the sores and rashes disappeared.

On November 13, 2022, Mexico voted in favor of the Palestinian cause and against Israel; a very bad decision. Archbishop invited us to do teshuva (repentance) for each nation that had chosen the same and to send an offering of restitution to honor Israel. In our congregation, when we sent a restitution offering, the blessing of the Father was poured out in our area, giving us abundant rains this winter season. The farmers are happy because they will now be able to sow the land without having to pay for irrigation water!

One Shabbat, a lady from the congregation testified of a miracle of healing from a large stone in her gallbladder. When she did the test, the stone was very large, and surgery was necessary. So she began to cry out to Yeshua for healing. (It is important to note that she is also a woman who constantly gives offerings of restitution.) After a week, she went to take some new tests, and to her great astonishment, the stone had disappeared. The doctor who did the examination spent much time trying to find the stone, but it was gone. Then she went to the doctor who was supposed to do the surgery, and he was amazed by this miracle. The doctor himself ended up crying, recognizing that it was Yeshua who did the miracle since she always speaks of His true name everywhere.

Another lady had some spots on her lungs, and she was told that she was in the terminal stage of her illness. She sent offerings of restitution to Israel, and after praying and believing the Father, she had repeat tests on her lungs, and they came out clean. She is now free of any symptoms of lung disease!

Another lady needed to apply for a visa for the USA since her daughter was there. She knew they were not issuing visas this year due to the pandemic. She began her paperwork last year, and the first miracle was that they gave her an appointment for October. Still, the visa took a long time to arrive, so she decided to give an offering of restitution in December. In eight days, she was informed that she should come in two weeks to pick up her new visa!

A lady, who had received Yeshua when Archbishop Dominiquae visited Mexico, gave a restitution offering to the ministry. A few months later, the Father opened the door for her to make the first payment for a lithium mine in Chile with an extension of 398 hectares!

In the first week of January, when the Omicron COVID variant was widespread in Mexico, my daughter and I became ill with the flu. We did not accept it as COVID. I know that the Key of Abraham works, so I sent an offering of restitution for Jahel and myself, and in just a week, we were fully recovered without any complications. I even received supernatural provision to go to the Sukkot Israel tour!

During the tour, we were shopping in Yardenit (the Jordan River baptismal site), and Rabbi did not have cash with him, so I paid his bill. Two days later, my account had doubled. Later on, we had an opportunity to give our first fruit, but this time I did not have cash with me. However, I decided to give a pledge of $200. After the tour, when I landed in Madrid, Spain on my way back to Mexico, I saw that I had received a deposit for fifty times the offering!

— Pastor Cesar Silva, Mexico

HEALING FROM COVID-19

I tested positive for COVID. I had caught it from my father and brother who had been infected. My pastor encouraged me to make restitution for my family, and I obeyed by giving the offering to UNIFY. The next day I felt better, and so did my father and brother. I regained my appetite and the fever left me. What a powerful restitution!

— Adina Lee, Hong Kong

Marriage Restored & Family Reconciliation

I felt that I needed to clean my parents-in-law's mossy gravestone as an act of restitution and to honor their memory. While doing that and remembering them, I began to repent of all my bitterness, hatred, and judgments against them and for not having honored them as my parents-in-law; therefore, I had not been able to honor my husband either. Right there, I understood that because they are my husband's parents, they are my parents, too! I began to thank Abba for them and started to bless their memory, and I also thanked Him for my husband.

Since then, there have been great changes: the inexplicable hatred and dissatisfaction with my husband, of which I have repented many times and from which I asked the Holy Spirit for deliverance, is finally broken. Hatred is gone, and love has filled my heart. When I started cleaning the gravestones, I could never have imagined what may follow! It is never too late; genuine love and mutual respect are now being restored to us after forty-four years of marriage.

Also, there was a rift between our adult children that had been going on for years, and reconciliation was very challenging because there was no communication between them. The situation was at an impasse even though we had prayed. I sent a restitution offering on behalf of my family to my Jewish mother, Archbishop Dominiquae, and a few weeks later, our children were suddenly reunited.

— Sinikka Backlund, Finland

GRI

When I started reading The Identity Theft, I realized that Jesus Christ, whom I had believed in for many years, is the Romanized Jesus Christ. I repented of that. Then I heard the teaching about the importance of repentance and making restitution. Once, after giving a restitution offering via UNIFY for the Ukrainian Jewish Aliyah on behalf of my country China, I saw in a dream three English letters: GRI. Immediately I enrolled in the GRI Against Anti-Semitism course to clear out the poisonous root of replacement theology and to become like Queen Esther who stood with her Jewish people.

— Shlomit Tang, Hong Kong

PROMOTION

After planting four palm trees in Gilgal through UNIFY, our daughter was promoted to a higher position; they did not even have a vacancy, but they created it for her. She received a pay rise of 4% while others were awarded just 2%. Four percent for four palm trees!

– Apostle Sana Enroos, Sweden

The More I Gave, the More I Received

I was greatly impacted by the message of restitution towards the Jewish people after reading *The Identity Theft* and studying the GRI course and GRM Bible school. *Restoration of Holy Giving* spoke especially to me. As a result, I reviewed all my finances and ensured that I was giving according to the Torah. This, I must confess, felt like a lot and only just about manageable. So, I was a bit stunned when there were requests for more voluntary offerings. I felt confused and wondered if Yah really wanted all this continual giving. But obviously He did, because He kept giving me the amounts that He wanted me to give!

So, although it hurt, I obeyed and said to myself, 'I will trust and not be afraid' (Isa 12:1–2). In my heart, I sensed I would be fine, even though prices everywhere in the UK were soaring and my family was sharing their financial difficulties with me. Then soon after, when I checked my inbox, there was an email telling me that I would receive an extra one and a half times my annual income on top of my regular yearly income! Wow! How wonderful is the Lord and how awesome His ways! I am so thankful to Him for the gift of restitution.

— Hilary Anderson, UK

New home

When we gave restitution offerings and gifts, danced, sang, and praised YHVH, we received great joy and anointing. I have never experienced that before. My husband and I have given restitution offerings to Jews and Israel by giving to UNIFY and sowing into different projects. Once in three days after sending an offering, we miraculously received a new rental home for which we had waited a long time. Victory in our finances! When we bless Israel and the Jews, YHVH blesses us according to Genesis 12:3. HalleluYah!

— Pernilla Kullander, Sweden

RESTITUTION AFFECTS THE MUSLIM GOVERNMENT

Eighteen members of our Malaysian team sent a restitution offering of $900 to UNIFY in November 2022. Before that, we made a trip to the prime minister's office in Putrajaya. It was raining heavily, and we managed to park our three vehicles adjacent to the main entrance of the office. Sitting in our cars, with Zoom linking us, we confessed and repented for our sin of Anti-MESITOJUZ and the sin of taking Israel (the land and the Jewish people) lightly by rejecting a diplomatic relationship with Israel and fighting for the Palestinian cause. In the end, we sounded our shofars calling for repentance.

A week later, Malaysia went into the fifteenth general election to vote for a new government. After the election I asked Abba, "Why have You chosen Mr. Anwar Ibrahim as Malaysia's tenth prime minister?" The answer came after I googled "Anwar Ibrahim and Israel" and found his statement about supporting efforts to protect the security of Israel during an interview with the Wall Street Journal in 2012. YHVH remembered what he said ten years back; the God of second chances gave him a second chance to fulfill his statement, as we, UNIFY Malaysia, made restitution and repentance on behalf of our country and the government for dishonoring Israel. Now he is the tenth prime minister of Malaysia. We keep praying for him to heed the call to stand with Israel.

— Pastor David Lee, Malaysia

FAMILY MIRACLES

I planted three date palms in Israel through UNIFY for my husband and two sons. The same day I sent the offering for the trees, my son received a holiday job offer, and two days later, my husband also received confirmation of his job promotion. When I saw that, I decided to sow two more date palms: one for my daughter and one for myself. Immediately my daughter was invited to a job interview. Later, when UNIFY sent our five tree-planting certificates, she received confirmation that she had received the job with that international company. Indeed, this is the power of Genesis 12:3 at work, as my children have sent out many job applications but had no success. They only received their breakthroughs when I sowed the seed on their behalf to UNIFY. My son's first-fruit offering from his holiday job was sent to UNIFY to purchase winter coats for Ukrainian immigrants in Nazareth. The next generation needs to understand the power of Genesis 12:3.

— Eunice Gware, PNG

Give, and it will be given to you—a good measure, pressed down, shaken together, overflowing, will be given into your lap. For whatever measure you measure out will be measured back to you.

Luke 6:38

UNIFY in Israel

Planting in Israel

In the generations to come Jacob will take root;
Israel will blossom and sprout, and they will fill the surface
of the world with fruit.

ISAIAH 27:6 AMP

We are reclaiming the covenant land of Israel back to its rightful owners, the Jewish people, by establishing UNIFY orchards in the biblical areas of Israel, and by teaming up with those that care for the land. Despite the enemy's plans, we are claiming the land of Abba with the Jewish people.

Olive Grove, Shavei Darom

United Nations for Israel planted an olive grove in Shavei Darom at the entrance to the Negev in 2021, just before the shmita year, partnering with the Jewish farmers. The residents of Shavei Darom are "the returnees of the South," those expelled from their village, Kfar Darom, in August 2005 during the infamous disengagement. After hellish suffering due to the injustice of USA and UN pressure on Israel to remove them from their land, they rebuilt themselves not far from Beer Sheva and called the community Shavei Darom. UNIFY planted this grove and is now also planting a memorial garden there as an act of restitution from the nations.

Fruit Orchard, Samaria

At the end of the *shmita* year in 2022, our Sukkot tour participants planted the UNIFY fruit orchard to support the Jewish community in the mountains of Samaria. This orchard was also dedicated as a prayer orchard in memory of Yuval, Archbishop Dominiquae and Rabbi Baruch Bierman's late son. UNIFY is also establishing a special lookout point called Mitzpeh Yuval, explaining the importance of this area where Shechem, Mount Gerizim, and Mt. Ebal are located. Since the planting, seven new families have moved in. Every Shabbat, the families bring their children to the orchard.

Date Palm Grove, Gilgal

In 2022, UNIFY planted date palms in Gilgal, near Jericho, where the children of Israel first entered the promised land. This date palm grove was planted for the redemption of the land of Israel.

This vineyard of 200 vines was planted by the members of

The United Nations for Israel

from many countries. 5783/2023

"In that day many nations will join themselves to A'donai
and they will be My people and I will dwell among you.'
Then you will know that A'donai-Tzva'ot has sent me to you."

Zechariah 2:15

Z30460

Vineyard, Samaria

In 2023, UNIFY assisted a Jewish farmer by planting a vineyard in Samaria. The Arabs, with the support of European money, had tried to claim land located in the mountains of Samaria from the Jewish state but, following the court case, the Israeli farmer was granted full rights to plant on this land. He needs all the help he can get to cultivate and make this land fruitful, and once he does so the land will remain in Israeli hands and be more easily defended.

Assisting in Aliyah

During 2022–2023, UNIFY helped the Ukrainian Jews to escape the warzone in Ukraine by supporting Ebenezer Operation Exodus[16] in bringing ten busloads of Ukrainian Jews to safety and helping them to make aliyah to Israel. UNIFY has also been assisting the local Messianic congregation in Israel that helps Ukrainian and Russian immigrants by donating finances for warm winter coats, blankets, and other necessities.

16   https://ebenezer-oe.org/

Sukkat Yehoshua in Ancient Gilgal

UNIFY established Sukkat Yehoshua, Joshua's tent of meeting, in ancient Gilgal in 2023. This special worship tent near the cave of Elijah and the location where Joshua led the Israelites into the promised land, is open for groups of believers to book for worship meetings. More information is at www.AncientGilgal.com.

The Watchman Apartment

UNIFY will soon have a special watchman apartment with the most epic view in the land, the Temple Mount! This will be our special watchman position for prophetic prayer and praise watches and shofar blowing in Jerusalem.

Support the Mission & Make Restitution

Unlock the Key of Abraham by responding to this message with your restitution offering.

- Donate to UNIFY to keep planting, building, and restoring the land of Israel with us!
- Support the watchman apartment
- **Support Jewish aliyah**
  UnitedNationsForIsrael.org/unify-donations/

Connect With Us

Visit our websites & follow us on social media

United Nations for Israel

Take a stand for the restoration of Israel and transform your nation into a sheep nation, one person at a time. Become a member and join our monthly members' online conferences to get equipped!

www.UnitedNationsForIsrael.org
info@unitednationsforisrael.org

Israel Tours

Travel through Israel on our "Bible Schools on Wheels" and watch the Hebrew Holy Scriptures come alive.

www.zionsgospel.com/tours-and-events/

Global Revival MAP (GRM) Israeli Bible Institute

Take the most comprehensive video Bible school online that focuses on the restoration of all things.

www.GRMBibleInstitute.com
info@grmbibleinstitute.com

Global Re-Education Initiative (GRI) Against Anti-Semitism

Discover the Jewish Messiah and defeat religious anti-Semitism! Order *The Identity Theft* and GRI Online Course Package

www.Against-Antisemitism.com
info@against-antisemitism.com

From Israel to the Nations TV Programs

Watch Archbishop Dominiquae Bierman's TV programs taped in the land of Israel!

Roku Channel: **Israel Revival**
YouTube: **Dominiquae Bierman TV**
www.youtube.com/@DominiquaeBiermanTV
Broadcasting Schedule: **www.zionsgospel.com/tv/**

MAP Prison Ministry

Through our prison ministry, pioneered by Rabbi Baruch Bierman, GRM Bible School is studied in prisons all over the USA. More information & to support:

www.zionsgospel.com/map-prison-ministry/

Sign our petition to ban neo-Nazi ideology in America and share it forward!

www.change.org/BanNeoNazism-Evil-Can-Be-Stopped

For more information about the founder of the ministries:

www.DominiquaeBierman.com

Books & Music

For more books by Dr. Dominiquae Bierman, order online: www.ZionsGospel.com

The Identity Theft
The Return of the 1st Century Messiah

"Yes!"
The dramatic life story of an Israeli woman who falls and rises again because of one word: "YES!"

Restoring the Glory – Volume I: The Original Way
The Ancient Paths Rediscovered

The MAP Revolution (free E-book)
Exposing theologies that obstruct the bride

Eradicating the Cancer of Religion
Hint: All People Have It!

The Healing Power of the Roots
It's a Matter of Life and Death!

Grafted In
It's Time to Return to Greatness!

Sheep Nations
It's Time to Take the Nations!

Yeshua is the Name
The Important Restoration of the True Name of the Messiah!

The Key of Abraham
The Blessing or the Curse?

Stormy Weather
Judgment Has Begun and Revival is Knocking at the Doors!

Restoration of Holy Giving
Releasing the True 1,000-Fold Blessing

The Bible Cure for Africa and the Nations
The key to the restoration of all Africa

Vision Negev
The Awesome Restoration of the Sephardic Jews!

Defeating Depression
This Book is a Kiss from Heaven!

From Sickology to a Healthy Logic
The product of 18 years walking through psychiatric
hospitals

Addicts Turning to God
The Biblical Way to Handle Addicts & Addictions

The Woman Factor: Freedom From Womanophobia
by Rabbi Baruch Bierman with Dominiquae Bierman

The Spider That Survived Hurricane Irma (free E-book)
God's call for America to repent

The Revival of the Third Day (free E-book)
The return to Yeshua the Jewish Messiah

Let's Get Healthy, Saints!
The Biblical Guide to Health

Tribute to the Jew in You Music Book
Notes for the Tribute to the Jew in You Music Album

Music Albums

Abba Shebashamayim
Uru
Retorno
The Key of Abraham
Tribute to the Jew in You
Tribute to the Jew in You Instrumental

Support the Mission

Contact Us

Archbishop Dr. Dominiquae & Rabbi Baruch Bierman
www.ZionsGospel.com | shalom@zionsgospel.com

Kad-Esh MAP Ministries

www.kad-esh.org | info@kad-esh.org

United Nations for Israel

www.unitednationsforisrael.org
info@unitednationsforisrael.org
52 Tuscan Way, Ste 202-412, St. Augustine,
Florida 32092, USA
+1-972-301-7087

APPENDIX II

Bibliography

Bierman, Dominiquae. *My Journey.* 4/23/2023. "My Journey" https://unitednationsforisrael.org/my-journey/

Bierman, Dominiquae. *The Identity Theft.* 2021. Zion's Gospel Press.

Luther, Martin. 1971. "On the Jews and Their Lies." Parts 11–13 in *Luther's Works: The Christian in Society IV, Vol. 47,* translated by Martin H. Bertram. Philadelphia: Fortress Press.

Made in the USA
Monee, IL
22 February 2024

53385301R00080